WITH THE GUNS IN THE PENINSULA

THE NAPOLEONIC LIBRARY

Other books in the series include:

WITH THE GUNS IN THE PENINSULA

THE PENINSULAR WAR JOURNAL OF CAPTAIN WILLIAM WEBBER, ROYAL ARTILLERY

Edited by Richard Henry Wollocombe

Preface by Lt-Colonel M.E.S. Laws, OBE, MC, RA

Frontline Books

Dedicated to Ellen Jane Wollocombe, 1791–1833
Sister of the Diarist and Great-great-grandmother of the Editor

With the Guns in the Peninsula

A Greenhill Book

Published in 1991 by Greenhill Books, Lionel Leventhal Limited
www.greenhillbooks.com

This edition published in 2017 by

Frontline Books
an imprint of Pen & Sword Books Ltd,
47 Church Street, Barnsley, S. Yorkshire, S70 2AS
For more information on our books, please visit
www.frontline-books.com, email info@frontline-books.com
or write to us at the above address.

ISBN: 978-1-47388-257-7

CIP data records for this title are available from the British Library

Printed and bound by CPI Group (UK) Ltd, Croydon, CR0 4YY

CONTENTS

CONTENTS Continued

ILLUSTRATIONS

Illustration sources

1: *History of the Life of Arthur, Duke of Wellington* Volume II, by M. Brialmont; 3, 4, 5 and 6: *The Life of the Most Noble Arthur, Marquis and Earl of Wellington* by Francis L. Clarke; 12: *The Artillerist's Manual of 1840*; 7: *British Battles on Land and Sea* by James Grant; 8: Miniature belonging to Mrs Mary Reed (neé Webber); 2: Print by J.A. Atkinson, courtesy of the Director, National Army Museum London; 9: Print by Dubourg, after Atkinson; 10: *History of the Dress of the Royal Regiment of Artillery 1625–1897* by Captain R.J. Macdonald RA; 13: *British Smooth-Bore Artillery* by Major-General B.P. Hughes, C.B., C.B.E.; 11: *Peninsular Sketches* by Actors on the Scene, Edited by W.H. Maxwell.

1. GENERAL SIR ROWLAND HILL, G.O.C., 2ND DIVISION.
Webber's Divisional Commander.

2. Artillery on the march - Torres Vedras, October 1810.

3. Battle of Talavera, 27 July 1809.
Webber viewed the battlefield on 27 September 1812.
See also Note 24 to Part I.

4. The Storming of Ciudad Rodrigo, January 1812.
Its capture, with that of Badajoz 3 months later, made possible
the Allied offensives of 1812 and 1813.

5. WELLINGTON'S ENTRY INTO MADRID, 12 AUGUST 1812.
Wellington wrote "I am among a people mad with joy"
Webber's journal for 6 June 1813 (final paragraph) testifies to this.

6. THE BATTLE OF SALAMANCA, 22 JULY 1812.
Evidence of the carnage of that former day is recorded by Webber
on 15 November 1812 as the Allied and French armies stood
once more face to face on the site of the battlefield.

7. SOULT BEFORE ALBA IN MID-NOVEMBER 1812.
Wellington declined to offer battle at this time, and the Journal recounts
the hasty and uncomfortable retreat into winter quarters that followed.

8. WILLIAM WEBBER, 2ND CAPTAIN THE ROYAL REGIMENT OF ARTILLERY.

9. Capture of General Edward Paget.
The incident is described in the Journal entry of 17 November 1812.

10. OFFICER OF FOOT ARTILLERY, 1812.
The Uniform worn by Webber at this time,
though the cocked hat was soon to be superseded by the Shako.

11. ARTILLERY IN THE HILLS

The steep descent to the Ebro (6 June 1813) and the snowy heights of
Roncesvalles (see Appendix II) were very difficult for artillery to negotiate.

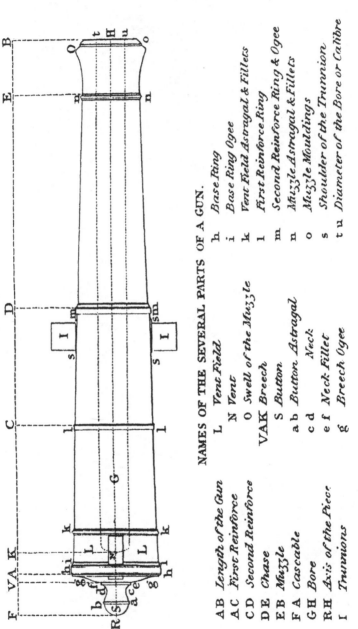

NAMES OF THE SEVERAL PARTS OF A GUN.

AB	Length of the Gun	L	Vent Field
AC	First Reinforce	N	Vent
CD	Second Reinforce	O	Swell of the Muzzle
DE	Chase	VAK	Breech
EB	Muzzle	S	Button
FA	Cascable	a b	Button Astragal
GH	Bore	c d	Neck
RH	Axis of the Piece	e f	Neck Fillet
I	Trunnions	g	Breech Ogee

h	Base Ring
i	Base Ring Ogee
k	Vent Field Astragal & Fillets
l	First Reinforce Ring
m	Second Reinforce Ring & Ogee
n	Muzzle Astragal & Fillets
o	Muzzle Mouldings
s	Shoulder of the Trunnion
t u	Diameter of the Bore or Calibre

12. A TYPICAL CAST PIECE.

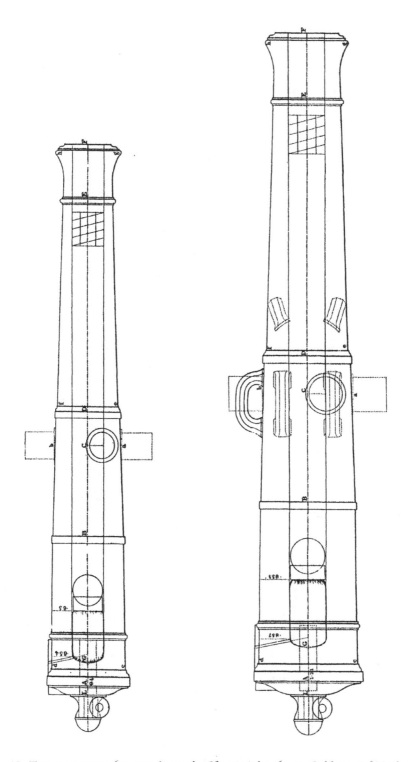

13. THE BRASS LIGHT 6PR GUN (Length: 5ft. Weight: 6cwt. Calibre: 3.688in)
and
THE BRASS 9 PR GUN (Length 5ft 11.4in. Weight: 13.5cwt. Calibre: 4.2in).

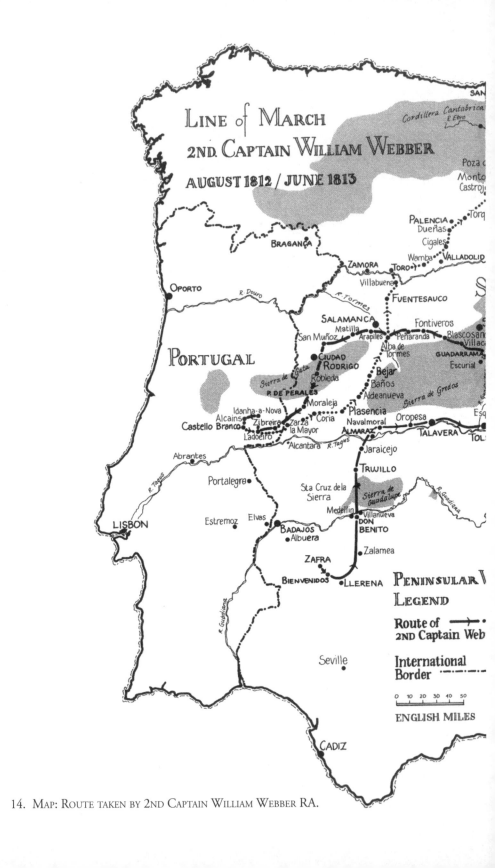

14. Map: Route taken by 2nd Captain William Webber RA.

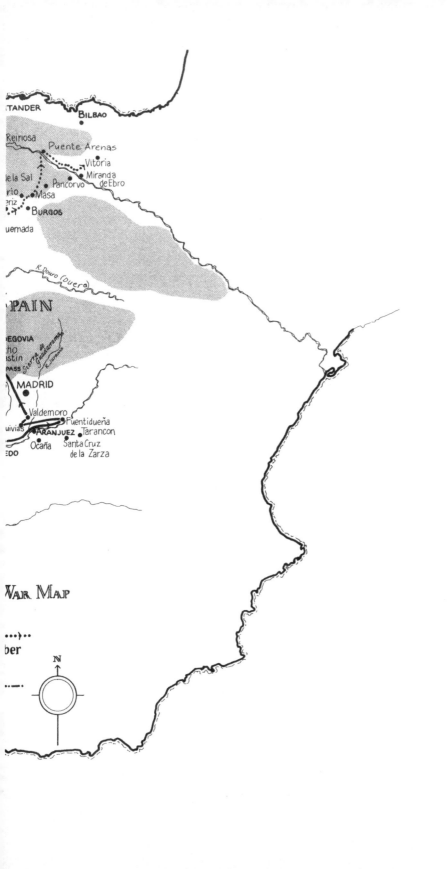

TANDER

BILBAO

Reinosa Puente Arenas

Vitoria

Miranda
de Ebro

de la Sal Pancorvo

rio Masa

riz

BURGOS

uemada

R. Douro (Duera)

PAIN

EGOVIA

ho

stin

PASS

MADRID

Valdemoro
Fuentidueña

uivas ARANJUEZ Tarancon

Ocaña Santa Cruz
de la Zarza

EDO

WAR MAP

•••┣••

ber

••━•

N

Editor's Introduction

LOOKING THROUGH some of my grandfather's notes recently, I came across his handwritten copy of a Journal of the Peninsular War, beginning in August 1812 and continuing into June 1813. Its author, William Webber, later to attain the rank of Brevet Lt-Colonel, was at the time of writing a 2nd Captain in the Royal Regiment of Artillery.

The present work has been undertaken in order to reproduce the Journal as it stands, adding other background information concerning the Colonel himself, the military campaign in which he was involved and something of Royal Artillery organization of the period. Copies of some contemporary letters and other documents of interest are included, in an appendix.

The text has been divided up into headed sections making, hopefully, for easier reading. Place names (as transcribed in my grandfather's hand, and not always easily readable) have been amended or brought up to date, where this has been thought necessary, or, in some instances, have been expanded to show the names in full. In the latter case, the expanded portions have been placed within square brackets. These portions, however, have generally been omitted from the Peninsular War map included in this volume, in the interests of space.

The following note was left by my grandfather; it serves to explain his access to the Journal and to the letters and documents mentioned above:

> The Battle of Vitoria was fought on the 21st June 1813. Going over the field afterwards, Colonel Webber picked up one of the notes issued in France in which French soldiers were paid. It is now with his papers in the possession of Wilmot and Rose Arundell, [of] Lifton Cottage (Jan 1915).

The Arundells were near neighbours of my grandfather, who was (as his father and grandfather had been in their times) rector of the adjacent Devon parish of Stowford. Both families were related to the Webbers through marriages with the Colonel's sisters.

The evident interest of these old papers prompted me to apply to the library of the Royal Artillery Historical Trust at the Old Royal Military Academy, Woolwich in order to enquire whether anything further was known about the author. My surprise was great on receiving their reply. It seemed that they themselves were in possession of a typed copy of the Journal and that it had been the subject of considerable research by the late Lt-Colonel M. E. S. Laws OBE, MC, RA, a well known historian of the Royal Artillery, who had not only annotated the text but had left some half dozen pages containing details of the Colonel's career and further commentary of a military nature. The content of his added note, signed and dated 21/6/1949, came as a further surprise; it read as follows:

> The original Journal of 2nd Captain Webber RA is the property of George E. Webber Esq of Winnipeg, by whose kind permission this typed copy has been taken for the RA Institution. In some cases the spelling of place names has been corrected.

I have been unable to trace the gentleman from Winnipeg or his heirs, although all seventeen Webbers listed in the telephone directory of that city have been sent letters of enquiry. Devon and Cornwall too (where the family traces its origins) have been searched without success for any trace of the Webber papers, while my last Arundell contact has retreated out to Australia. I have therefore not been able to view the original of the Journal. I believe, however, that both the RA Historical Trust's typed copy and my grandfather's handwritten one were taken from it. If this is the case, then at some time between 1915 and 1949 it would seem that the original, and no doubt the rest of Colonel Webber's papers, have changed both custodian and continent; but how this happened, where they are now and who has them must remain something of a mystery.

The interest and any historical value the Journal may have derive as much from its illumination of the personality and outlook of a junior officer in Wellington's army as from any new insight it affords into grand strategy or the conduct of military operations. The few known circumstances and recollections of Colonel Webber's background and life are therefore set out below in this introduction. Details of his army career, explanations as to the progress of operations and other information on military matters are contained in the preface, in the introductory sections to each part of the text and in the notes at the end of the work - the greater part of these being the fruits of Colonel Laws' professional expertise and research.

I am also indebted to Brigadier K. A. Timbers, Historical Secretary of the Royal Artillery Historical Trust, and his staff in the library at Woolwich for their help, and to the Royal Artillery Institution for letting me use the library at Woolwich and permitting the publication of material found there.

*

William Webber was born on 28th May 1787, the eldest child of another William Webber and his wife, Jane Frances, daughter and co-heir of Ralph Winstanley Wood of Wigan (Lancs) and Pierrepont in Farnham, Surrey.

This Mr Wood, originally of the 8th Dragoons, travelled out to India as a cornet in the same ship as Warren Hastings. Advised by the latter, he left the Army and set about amassing a large fortune as a salt agent to the East India Company. The marriage of his daughter Jane Frances to Mr Webber senior took place on 15th August 1786, when she was only 15 years old, in the chapel of Farnham Castle. The bishop of Winchester officiated, one of the witnesses being Frederick North (probably the Prime Minister).

The Webbers came of an old Cornish family, bearing arms and at the end of the sixteenth century living at Amell in the parish of St Kew. Digorie Webber, a third son living in the mid-seventeenth century, embarked on what was to become something of a family tradition of Indian service: he commanded an East Indiaman and his son John enlisted in the East India Company. John's son William,

25

however, (the Colonel's grandfather) took to the law, being called to the bar of the Inner Temple in 1750, where he is said to have declined the offer to become Master of its Bench. His son, yet another William (the Colonel's father), reverted to the family's Indian tradition, becoming Chief Secretary in the government of Bengal under both Warren Hastings and Cornwallis. Honourable East India Company records show him to have been born at Shinfield in Berkshire in 1755. He died in 1832, his wife, Jane Frances, predeceasing him by eight years. Latterly they had lived at Hexworthy House, Lawhitton, near Lifton. They were buried alongside each other in nearby Stowford.

Colonel Webber had three brothers and two sisters; George joined the Navy and attained the rank of Commander; Edward died young; Frederick graduated from Pembroke College, Oxford and after serving as a chaplain in India became rector of St Michael Penkevil in Cornwall, a position he held for thirty-seven years. The elder sister, Mary Lucinda, married W. A. Harris Arundell of Lifton Park, a large landowner and dignitary of the counties of Devon and Cornwall. The younger sister, Ellen Jane, married John Wollocombe, rector of Stowford - and since their son (my great-grandfather) married Mary Lucinda's daughter, i.e. his first cousin, I myself bear a double portion of the Webber genes. The Webbers were said to have been deaf (cp the Journal entry for 9th March 1813) and certainly my family have until recently been much afflicted with this disease.

Colonel Webber's childhood was probably passed in Exmouth, but when just fifteen years old he was placed with the Old Royal Military Academy at Woolwich as a gentleman cadet. The Royal Regiment of Artillery, into which he graduated, required its officers to be sufficiently well educated to carry out their professional duties - a requirement nicely reflected in the style and content of the Journal, which reads generally with clarity and freshness.

That he is a child of his times and background is very clear. Brought up in England during a period that has been described as a golden age of reason and refinement, he feels himself well able to view the foreign scene with a discriminating eye, and his reflections on Iberian life and customs are delightfully candid. As a member of the Established

Church too, he finds some of their Popish habits hard to countenance: the strict incarceration of young women in nunneries for instance; he is particularly (and possibly not totally disinterestedly) exercised on this subject.

In August 1812, when Webber joined Sir Rowland Hill's Corps in the Peninsula, the army had been campaigning there for some years, and the Journal is well stocked with comment from the already familiar political and social scene - the customary depredations of the French (who are, however, worthy foes), the wretched state of the Spaniards and, regrettably, the inferiority of the Portuguese.

The Journal tells of long marches, of dragging the guns (they were 9-pounders) over difficult terrain, of rain and cold, the heat of the sun and arrivals at bivouacs without firewood or food. The British army's stomach was not well provided for during the earlier part of the campaigns described. Communications, however, were surprisingly good, judging by the informed comment about army plans and the dispositions of the enemy.

Webber finds plenty to entertain himself during the campaigning. The pages of the Journal are filled with remarks on a range of subjects, which lends variety to the daily account of military movements and operations: church architecture, painting, music, the theatre, balls, dinner parties and female beauty (particularly the latter) are examples.

He finds many opportunities for indulging his passion for riding, often combining duties for reconnaissance and foraging with time off for recreation and sight-seeing. And if the 'taste' exhibited by Spanish decorative arts does not always meet with his approval, perhaps he may be excused - at least he is interested in what he sees and, after all, he is only twenty-five years old and giving a pretty good account of himself. Jane Austen would have been proud of him! And what better standard had he to go by, in any case, than English architecture and art of the eighteenth century?

The army in the Peninsula, in respect of its officers at any rate, comes across as something in the nature of an exclusive club. Webber sometimes dines well - on occasions with his corps commander, Sir

Rowland Hill, though there is no record of an invitation from the latter to follow his pack of hounds. The other ranks, it must be said, are seldom mentioned and one feels that their lot would have been monotonous in the extreme, relieved only by infrequent bouts of drunkenness that sometimes brought down upon them the wrath of their respected leader. Lord Wellington is mentioned in terms that seem to set him on a level with the Lord Buddha.

Webber's brother officers and friends include earlier contemporaries at Woolwich and former companions in arms, many of whom were to be with him at Waterloo - Whinyates and Beane (his Waterloo commander) for example. Maxwell, the commander of his brigade of 9-pounders, is mentioned most often.

Stewart Maxwell was commissioned some five years before Webber and was promoted Captain in 1810. He is gazetted in 1817 as a Major dating from 1814 and possessing two medals and the Order of the Bath. He died in May 1824. His younger brother, incidentally, who retired as Colonel Montgomery Maxwell K.H. of the 36th Regiment, was serving at this time in the Artillery in Italy (Calabria) and subsequently published *My Adventures* in the form of Letters written on active service. One of these is addressed to "'S', serving with the army in Spain" (probably his brother Stewart).

Stewart Maxwell may have provided something of a pattern for the younger Webber to emulate, the former's trial by court martial during the period notwithstanding. He seems to have been an urbane fellow and a popular commander - witness the cheers of his men when he returns to the brigade after being acquitted.

Full details of Webber's career are contained in the preface. The arrival of his unit (D Troop RHA, commanded by Major Beane) on the battlefield of Waterloo is attested by Captain Cavalié Mercer in his celebrated *Journal of the Waterloo Campaign*, when he writes: 'Just outside the hedge I found Major Beane's [Webber's unit], which had arrived during the night direct from England.'

Captain Mercer was Webber's troop commander for a short time in 1816 and, when returning from leave with his wife in February of that year, met some officers from his Company on the roadside at St

Denis. He writes as follows, showing Webber's health to have been still far from robust:

> Frazer and Ambrose [Assistant Surgeon mentioned also in Webber's journal] rode up. From them we learned that old Webber had made my house very comfortable in Stain [on the outskirts of Paris]. Webber had hired some little shabby furniture...

Mercer's wife did not find it very comfortable however. When the party was ready to continue on the march towards Boulogne and eventual repatriation, 2nd Captain Webber said he was too weak to leave and so had to be left in Ambrose's care.

One other little anecdote about the Colonel may be recounted here. It is taken from my great-grandfather's memoirs, *From Morn till Eve.*

> After the Oxford Commemoration [ca.1843] I returned home for the long vacation, during which I accompanied my aunt and sisters to Bude, a seaside place on the North coast of Cornwall, where my brother was reading before he entered the Army; and here we were joined by our uncle, Colonel Webber of the Artillery who had served at Corunna and throughout the Peninsular War and also at Waterloo. In person and feature he resembled the Duke of Wellington, and had on several occasions been mistaken for him in the undress blue frock and cocked hat of the Artillery - the usual costume of their great leader. He was one of the best riders in the service, and conquered horses that rough riders could not...
> One day, during his visit to Bude, as we were entering the town of Stratton, he said to my brother, "Now I will show you how to defend a town and dispute the enemy's entrance."
> Going on ahead of us he disappeared round the corner of a house, his uniform a long blue mackintosh, and his weapon an umbrella. As we drew near his lurking place, he sprang out into the street, fired at us, and then retreated at a run, loading his umbrella as he went; he again ensconced himself behind some sheltering angle and repeated his

attack on us, fired, and then scurried away, biting off the end of his cartridge and ramming the load home as he made for another post of vantage.

Colonel Webber never married. He settled down in the west country and died at Hexworthy House, Lawhitton, the residence of his brother George, on 1st March 1847. He was buried at Stowford beside his parents. A tablet in the church briefly records his military service.

Preface
WEBBER'S MILITARY CAREER
BY LT-COLONEL M. E. S. LAWS OBE, MC, RA

{The detailed account of Webber's military career which follows, and which was written by Colonel Laws, has been added to by the inclusion of a few paragraphs on the organization of the allied army in the Peninsula and on the composition and armament of artillery units of the day.}

William Webber obtained a cadetship in the Royal Artillery on 9th June 1801 and was duly commissioned as 2nd Lieutenant on 8th September 1803. On joining at Woolwich he was posted to Captain J. Sheldrake's Company, Third Battalion RA,[1] which was then stationed at Colchester, but he never in fact joined the unit, being retained at Headquarters, probably for further training. Owing, however, to the very rapid expansion of the regiment under the stimulus of the long war with France, there was a serious shortage of officers, with a resulting quickening of promotion, so that on 6th December 1803 he was gazetted Lieutenant and was posted to a vacancy in the Seventh Battalion RA.[2]

At that time four of the ten companies of the Seventh Battalion were serving in the West Indies and the remaining six companies were in Ireland. Accordingly Lieutenant Webber embarked at Woolwich on the transport *Eclipse* on 12th December 1803 with a draft of 105 other ranks of the Royal Artillery. On board the same ship was Lt-Colonel E. Stehelin (534)[3] who was going out to the West Indies to take up the appointment of Commander Royal Artillery in the Windward and Leeward Islands. The ship ran into very heavy weather in the Channel and put into Plymouth about the end of January 1804, having had two men swept overboard. Eventually the draft landed at Barbados on 21st March 1804, when Webber was posted to Captain

(Brevet Major) W. Wilson's [4] Company, Fourth Battalion RA.[5]

The garrison of Barbados was at that time only waiting for the arrival of drafts from England to despatch an expeditionary force under Major-General Sir Charles Green against the Dutch colony of Surinam. This force left Barbados on 2nd April 1804, the Royal Artillery component consisting of six officers (including Lieutenant Webber) and ninety-eight other ranks, made up of small detachments from no less than seven different companies of Royal Artillery. The operations were entirely successful and though there was not much fighting, there was a great deal of heavy labour for all ranks in a notoriously trying climate and in very difficult country. Movements of formed bodies of troops were in fact confined to the rivers Surinam and Commewyne, for the country was marshy and covered with thick jungle. On 5th May the Dutch capitulated and the British then withdrew to Barbados a few days later, leaving a small garrison to hold the conquered colony. Lieutenant Webber was wounded, but not severely, during the operations and was fortunate in returning to Barbados in May 1804.

Though his wound was not serious, the young officer nearly died of the dreaded yellow fever, and early in August the Commander Royal Artillery at Barbados wrote to the Deputy Adjutant General RA at Woolwich as follows:

> I have had to apply for a Medical Board on Lieutenant Webber in consequence of which the Commander of the Forces has been pleased to grant him six months' leave of absence to return to Europe for the benefit of his health. This young man has never been well since his return from the Expedition to Surinam where Major Wilson had an opportunity of seeing his conduct and speaks of it in high terms. As it is necessary that he should take the very first opportunity (to go home) by the Packet in order to save his life, which will occasion him much expense, I have advised him to make application through you either to the Master General [of the Ordnance] or to the Board, whichever you may judge proper, and hope you will interest yourself in obtaining for him some allowance for his passage. His conduct while with me has been extremely correct.[6]

Whether in fact any ex gratia payment was ever made to cover the cost of a packet passage is not now known, but the kindly recommendation of his CRA was probably not without effect on his professional career.

Lieutenant Webber therefore embarked aboard the packet *Duke of Cumberland*, still desperately ill and confined to his bunk. Four days later the ship was driven ashore in St John's Bay, Antigua, during a violent storm and became a total loss, but the invalid survived a night exposed on deck to torrential rain and was fortunate to be rescued next day before the ship broke up; he lost all his kit however. Eventually he got a passage in another ship and reached England about mid-November 1804 for his six months' sick leave.

At the end of his leave, Lieutenant Webber was posted from Captain C. Gold's Company[7], Seventh Battalion RA - to which he had been posted in August 1804 on leaving the West Indies but which in fact he never joined - to Captain Fraser's Company, Eighth Battalion RA at Woolwich.[8] In May 1806 this company moved from Woolwich to Warley and in the following month Lieutenant Webber was posted to D Troop, Royal Horse Artillery [9] at the same station. As the Royal Horse Artillery was considered a *corps d'élite* and appointment to its units was greatly sought after, it seems probable that Webber was indebted to the favourable report of his CRA in the West Indies for this posting. He did not long remain with D Troop however, for in August 1807 he was transferred to C Troop RHA [10] at Woolwich. In November 1807 he moved with his troop from Woolwich to Warley and there remained until early October 1808. He appears to have recovered his health, since he had no leave since joining C Troop and was shown month after month on the muster rolls as being at duty.

On 5th October 1808 Lieutenant Webber - by then the second senior subaltern of C Troop RHA - embarked with his unit at Northfleet for active service in northern Spain with Lt-General Sir David Baird's division which was ordered abroad to reinforce Sir John Moore's army based on Lisbon. B Troop RHA [11] also formed part of Baird's force, which took some time to collect. C Troop did not sail from the Downs till the last day of October. After a fine passage, C Troop arrived at Corunna on 8th November and landed two days later. On 18th November the troop marched from Corunna towards the French frontier to make contact with Sir John Moore's army, then about Salamanca.

It was a very difficult march over villainous roads. On the second day, for example, Captain Evelegh and Lieutenant Webber spent five hours bringing in a single wagon for the last three miles of a twenty-mile march. By end-November the troop had reached Bembibre, some 105 miles from Corunna as the crow flies but far more by the road, when orders were received to retire. For the next nine days the troop retraced its steps, reaching Guitiriz (thirty miles from Corunna) when it received new orders to advance once more. Again the eastward march was resumed, and by 20th December C Troop had reached Valderas, just too late to take part in the cavalry action at Sahagun next day.

On 23rd December Lieutenant Webber suffered very painful injuries to his face when his horse came down on the frozen road, and though he continued at duty he was badly shaken and in considerable pain. The troop was present at the affair at Benavente on 29th December, but was not engaged; it continued with B Troop to support the cavalry in covering the retreat of the army till it reached Corunna at 7 pm on 10th January 1809, after a series of terrible marches in deep snow and largely without food or shelter. C Troop had several times been in action during the retreat, notably at Cacabellos on 3rd January and Constantino on 5th January.

Webber was still a very sick man and was evidently unfit for duty, so that most of the rearguard work during the retreat fell on the other officers of the troop. C Troop embarked all its men, guns and horses on 11th January and was not present at the battle on 16th January. It had marched 800 miles between 18th November and 10th January and had lost over 80 horses from exhaustion and exposure.

C Troop reached Plymouth at 5 pm on 23rd January and there landed and marched via Reading to Woolwich. Webber was at once

34

sent on sick leave till April, but he then rejoined his unit at Woolwich and there remained at duty till 1812. On 17th April 1812 he was promoted 2nd Captain [12] and was posted to Captain S. Maxwell's Company,[13] Fourth Battalion RA, serving in the Peninsula as a field battery of 9-pounders with Lt-General Hill's 2nd Division.

The company had been raised as Captain W. Martin's Company, Fourth Battalion RA on 1st January 1771, and had been in America from June 1773 (mostly at Boston and at New York) till 1783, when it moved to St John's, Newfoundland. In September 1786 it reached Woolwich and served there and at Chatham and Portsmouth till 1793, when it went to Flanders for the campaign under the Duke of York, returning to Woolwich from north Germany in May 1795. It was equipped as a field battery and stationed at Ringmer (Sussex) till 1802 and then moved to Leith Fort and later to Haddington. In 1807 the company took part in the expedition to the River Plate before returning to Woolwich in February 1808, to be stationed later at Exeter, until 1810.

On 30th September 1810 the company, commanded by Captain J. Hawker, embarked at Portsmouth on the transport *Eliza* and landed at Lisbon on 23rd October. It was equipped as a field battery near Lisbon during the winter months and took its full share of the 1811 campaign under Marshal Beresford, being present at the fierce battle of Albuera and at the first and second sieges of Badajoz. The company wintered at Portalegre and Castello Branco and arrived at Zafra in about July 1812, where shortly afterwards Webber joined it.

Wellington's army in the Peninsula was one of mixed nationalities. Besides the British, who were the most numerous, there were important elements from the continent - Hanoverians of the King's German Legion, Brunswickers of the Oels and Hussars regiments, French royalists of the Chasseurs Britanniques, and Portuguese (principally infantry and artillery), who had been trained under Beresford and comprised some two-fifths of the total strength.

The organization of the army was as follows: there were two divisions of cavalry, seven of infantry of the line, and one of light infantry under General Craufurd. Divisions of infantry of the line contained typically three brigades, of which one would be Portuguese. There was in addition a further Portuguese division (Hamilton's) and two separate Portuguese brigades. Infantry divisions had one or two field batteries under command. The cavalry, most often operating as independent brigades, were supported by troops of horse artillery.

The 2nd Division, consisting of one Portuguese and three British brigades and, with Hamilton's Portuguese and (by end October 1812) Colonel Skerret's Brigade from Cadiz in support, was employed as a detached force under the overall command of General Hill. At the disposal of this force were two Portuguese and two British field batteries (of which Captain Maxwell's was one).

It should be understood that at this time companies of the Royal Artillery were not permanently equipped for any particular role. To produce a field battery, all that was considered necessary was to issue the appropriate guns (usually 9-pounders) and wagons to a selected company RA and to attach to it a small detachment of men and horses of the Royal Artillery Drivers corps. The complete augmented unit was then officially designated 'Captain —'s Company of the — Battalion RA manning a Brigade of guns', or more shortly 'Captain —'s Brigade', or 'Captain —'s 9-Pounder Brigade'.

A field battery or brigade differed substantially in this regard from a troop of the Royal Horse Artillery: the latter had its own horses and drivers, which were part of the unit and which remained permanently with it, while the horses and drivers of a field battery belonged to a separate corps and were commanded and administered by officers of that corps. Whereas the Royal Horse Artillery, since its inception in 1793, had been regarded as a *corps d'élite*, which accepted only specially selected officers and men from the Royal Artillery and which trained always for one particular task, a company of Royal Artillery might find itself manning the seaward defences of Portsmouth one day and acting as a field battery the next. Furthermore the Royal Horse Artillery never served abroad, except when required to do so on active service.

The strength of a troop of RHA in the field varied in practice considerably from perhaps 170 up to 250 officers and men. A company of Royal Artillery, following the establishment of 1782, was to consist of a Captain and 2nd Captain, two Lieutenants, one 2nd Lieutenant and 110 other ranks, of which some 16 were intended to be tradesmen - i.e. carpenters, smiths, collar makers, wheelers, a tailor and two drummers. In addition, there would be the required complement of Royal Artillery Drivers - on the scale of one officer, one quartermaster, three NCOs and 26 Privates.

The muster roll of Captain Maxwell's Company, taken at Alcains on 9th January 1813, gives the names of one Captain, one 2nd Captain, one 1st Lieutenant, one 2nd Lieutenant, 4 Sergeants, 4 Corporals, 9 Bombardiers, 96 Gunners and 3 Drummers. However, only fifty-nine of all ranks were recorded as present. By July the total strength had risen to 121 officers and men, but only fifty-three were present. Those missing were marked 'Sick', 'Lisbon', 'England', or 'Command', the latter signifying a secondment to divisional duties outside the company.

The armament of a field brigade of Royal Artillery, such as Captain Maxwell's, was most often 9-pounders - five of them plus one heavy 5.5-inch howitzer. A troop of RHA at the beginning of the Peninsular War might be equipped with either two 9-pounders or two heavy 6-pounders, together with three light 6-pounders and one heavy 5.5-inch howitzer; it would have some six ammunition waggons and four other carriages. Before Waterloo, however, in order to match the weight of the French artillery, many troops of the RHA were re-equipped with 9-pounders. The guns were fitted up with the newly-developed General Congreve block trailer, which allowed them to be manoeuvred more easily and, consequently, laid with greater accuracy than was formerly possible.

The effective point blank range of a 9-pounder with a 3-lb charge was 300 yards. A two degree elevation of the gun extended the range to 1,000 yards; a further degree to 1,400 yards. The accuracy was something like plus or minus 10%. Surprisingly rapid rates of fire could be achieved by means of the efficient gun drill of the day - as high as one round at ten second intervals if so desired, for instance when firing at advancing infantry at point blank range.

Three types of ammunition were in use: solid round-shot, canister-shot (each canister carrying forty-one 5-oz bullets), and spherical case containing a large number of bullets together with a bursting fuse. The amount of each type carried in the field was generally based on the proportion 70% round-shot, to 11.5% canister-shot and 18.5% spherical case.

Horses to drag all this equipment were required in large numbers and were invariably in short supply. Imported animals were preferred when they could be obtained, as local horses and mules were found to be of poor quality. Teams of eight were employed to enable the RHA to deploy and retire their 9-pounders (with a weight behind the guns of 38 cwt) at speed. Many more were required for the ammunition wagons, for other carriages and as mounts for officers.

2nd Captain Webber's Journal opens on 28th August 1812, which may well be the date on which he joined Captain Maxwell's Brigade, and continues till 16th June 1813. The Journal was written on odd pieces of paper, not in a book, and appears to have been entered up daily except in a few cases where entries for two or three days have clearly been made at the same time. There are unfortunately a few gaps, possibly owing to sheets having been lost. It is clear that part of the Journal after 16th June 1813 has indeed been lost, since it ceases abruptly in the middle of a sentence and most tantalisingly does not include the battle of Vitoria on 21st June.

Yet despite these imperfections the Journal gives a very interesting and almost daily record of the detached force under Lt-General Sir Rowland Hill's command. Few diaries kept by regimental officers of the Royal Artillery during the Peninsular campaign have survived and this is the only one kept by a Gunner officer of the 2nd Division.

The Journal is remarkably accurate in its record of current events witnessed by the writer and has been checked against the monthly muster rolls and pay lists [14] of the unit for matters of internal detail. It is valuable as evidence of the day to day life of a field battery on active service no less than as a record of the reactions of an average regimental officer to the contemporary manners and customs of Spanish and

Portuguese society.

Though the Journal ends on 16th June 1813, it is known that Webber took part in the battle of Vitoria and subsequently in the battles of the Pyrenees (July 1813), the Nive (December 1813), Orthez (February 1814) and Toulouse (April 1814).[15] There is, however, little detailed information concerning his experiences during these later campaigns. Some idea of the severity of the conditions under which the fighting went on in the Pyrenees in the winter of 1813-1814 may be judged from an incident he records in a 'Statement of Services' (a copy of which is included in the appendix).

As soon as the fighting in southern France ceased, Captain Maxwell went to England on leave and it fell to Webber as 2nd Captain to take the company to Canada where the war with the United States was still in progress. The unit embarked at Bordeaux at the end of May 1814 and reached Quebec about 1st August 1814, moving to Chambly in September. Finding that there was no opportunity for active service in Canada, Webber obtained six months' leave and returned to England, sailing from Quebec on board the transport Mariner on 11th September and arriving at Woolwich about 2nd November.

On the recommendation of his old divisional commander he was appointed as 2nd Captain to D Troop RHA in June 1815. This troop was commanded by Captain George Beane and had been serving alongside Captain Maxwell's Brigade during the 1812-1813 compaigns in the Peninsula. It was also the unit to which Webber had been posted on his first appointment to the Royal Horse Artillery as a subaltern.

D Troop RHA had only recently returned from southern France when it was ordered to Flanders to join the Duke of Wellington's army. 2nd Captain Webber joined it just as it was about to embark, and the troop reached the Allied army just in time to take part in the decisive battle of Waterloo. D Troop was allotted to the Reserve Artillery, but came into action early in the battle when the first attack was made on La Haye Sainte and was very heavily engaged all day.[16] Towards the end of the battle, Webber's horse was killed by a shell while at a full gallop and the rider was very heavily thrown. Though untouched by shell splinters, he received severe contusions on one side of the body as well as internal injuries. He was removed to Brussels where he slowly recovered. [17]

Very shortly after Webber had been wounded, Captain Beane was killed and the command of the troop devolved on a subaltern. As Webber had not actually commanded the troop at any time on 18th June, he was not included in the list of brevet promotions with which unit commanders were rewarded after Waterloo.[18] On the matter being brought to official notice by a petition however, he was appointed Brevet Major on 21st January 1819.

After recovery from his wound, 2nd Captain Webber rejoined D Troop RHA [19] in France, but on the troop being disbanded on 31st July 1816, he was transferred to F Troop RHA [20] commanded by Captain J. Webber Smith (subsequently Lt-General, but no relative to William Webber so far as is known) and stationed at Woolwich and later at Ringmer. But there was great stagnation in promotion and Webber was not in good health, so in August 1826 he took advantage of the special terms offered to RA officers and retired on the Unattached List with the half pay of a Major. In January 1837 he was given the brevet of Lieutenant-Colonel on the Unattached List and at once offered his services in view of the troubles in Spain; his offer was suitably acknowledged but nothing further came of it.

Part One
The Advance to Aranjuez

DURING THE Summer of 1812 Wellington with the bulk of the Anglo-Portugese army had been operating about Salamanca, leaving Lt-General Sir Rowland Hill with a detached force (of which Captain S. Maxwell's 9-Pounder Brigade formed part) to hold the Tagus valley. On 22nd July Wellington decisively defeated Marmont at Salamanca and drove the disorganised French army of Portugal northwards beyond Valladolid. King Joseph, alarmed for the safety of his capital, ordered Soult to raise the siege of Cadiz, evacuate Andalucia and retire to Toledo.

Wellington then marched on Madrid which he entered on 12th August without opposition from King Joseph, who retired to Valencia. As soon as it was evident that Soult was in fact evacuating Andalucia, Wellington ordered Hill's detached force to move forward to the area south of Madrid, while he himself with the main army moved northwards towards Valladolid to deal with Clausel, who had replaced Marmont in command of the French army of Portugal. The advance of General Sir Rowland Hill's force is described in the first part of Captain Webber's Journal.

Journal of a March with
Lt-General Sir Rowland Hill's Corps
from Zafra in Spain
Commencing August 28th 1812

ZAFRA TO DON BENITO

August 28

A T 3 THIS morning we marched right in front to Bienvenida, distant 4 leagues. The first two miles of the road as far as [Puebla de] Sancho Parez almost too bad for four-wheeled carriages. However, ours stood the shaking well and no delay occurred. Afterwards we entered an open good road leading through a plain, which continued all the way. At 9 we arrived, formed our park near a convent, picketed our horses and put our sick men into the chapel.

At the same hour the Brigades from Los Santos and Almendral arrived. The latter had moved the night before to some cantonment in the neighbourhood of Los Santos. These were preceded by a few Dragoons of the Royals, and the whole took up their ground on a hill to the right of the town under the shade of an olive plantation.

I dined with Sir Rowland Hill, who of course with his Staff had the best house in the place. After an excellent dinner and the best of wines - Madeira, Port and Claret - I took leave.

At dinner the General received dispatches from some Spaniard in Seville giving intelligence of Col Kemp's having taken a fort with some magazines on the road to that place and that he was marching direct for it and expected to enter in a day or two - a Captain of Artillery was killed in this affair with the enemy and Col Downie [1] who was in command of the Corps of Spanish cavalry has been defeated, his whole Corps killed, taken or dispersed and himself badly wounded and a prisoner.

Some time ago Soult, in his dispatch to Joseph Buonaparte mentioned in an insignificant manner that he met some 'Spanish Comedians' (meaning the cavalry alluded to) and not knowing what to make of them, sent his grenadiers to send them about their

43

business, on which he said they fled like sheep. Several of our officers have seen them and agree with Soult that they had the appearance of a party of strolling players, from the singularity of their dress.

Maxwell [2] and myself passed the night in the orchestra of the chapel. The other officers of the Brigade had a better place in a room behind the altar. There is nothing worth notice in Bienvenida except the tower of the church, the architecture of which is very peculiar. The town is badly supplied with water and the little to be found in the tanks at this season is unwholesome.

August 29

At half past three this morning we formed close column, right in front, on the road to Llerena and at 4 marched, preceded by a Squadron of the Royals. The road was good and level. On the right is a ridge of hills which extend for a considerable distance towards Seville. Our course is to the eastward and we are at present at a loss to imagine where we are going. After a march of three leagues we reached Llerena, a large town which afforded quarters for us all. Our houses were in a convent and the men in houses near it. The French had only left the place the day before.

I walked about the town but saw nothing remarkable except the Cathedral,[3] the interior of which is handsomely ornamented and contains an excellent organ. I dined with Captain Egerton of the 34th Regiment and in the evening walked with him into the grand square, the usual promenade for people of all classes.

August 30

At 4 we were joined by several squadrons of Cavalry, which had been encamped near the town during the night, and marched for Burguillos [?] preceded by them and the 3rd Regt or Buffs. As information had arrived that part of the enemy's rearguard occupied ground nearby we expected to see something of them, but did not.

Our march was over level ground, well cultivated in several spots. At 2.5 leagues from Llerena we arrived at Ahillones, a small village half a league from Berlanga, and one Brigade of Infantry and ours of

Artillery were halted there. The others with the Cavalry went on to the latter place. We got our men and horses under cover, though they were much crowded. Nothing particular at Ahillones.

August 31

At 4 we marched for Maguilla, out of our direction to enable the rear of the Corps to enter Ahillones. The distance 2 leagues by a good road through cornfields and the country open and level. We passed through Maguilla and encamped a mile and a half the other side in a valley under the shade of several olive trees. In the evening the Infantry, which had marched the day before to Berlanga joined us, but the Cavalry had been ordered to their different Regiments which were on our right, a small force of the enemy being in that direction.

September 1

At 4 we marched for Campillo de Llerena, 4 leagues distant, by a very bad road, in some parts almost impassable. The Infantry went another way, a league shorter but only passable for them. The country more hilly and enclosed and several mountains were seen at a distance in this day's march. We encamped at Campillo de Llerena, or rather in some fields near it. Headquarters were established there and the staff occupied all the houses. Water very scarce, muddy and bad.

September 2

At half past three marched for Zalamea [de la Serena] by a very bad road, 4.5 leagues distant. That taken by the Infantry 3.5 but merely a goat walk and I understand made the march more fatiguing than it would have been by our road. We had good quarters in Zalamea, which is a large village. The Portuguese however were obliged to encamp on some ground near it - the bells were ringing and continued doing so for the whole day. Headquarters at this place.

September 3

At 4 we marched for Quintana de la Serena, 2 leagues - the Portuguese to Castuera, 3 leagues at which our Headquarters were to be this day. We came through a wood of olives and other trees by a good road and were able to get quarters for all our men. The horses were picketed in a garden. The town is well supplied with good water and plenty of forage is to be found in the neighbourhood.

The approach to the village is very pretty and indeed the village itself is so when seen from the country within a mile of it on either side. Vineyards, olive groves and fruit gardens surround it. The houses are bad and not one pretty woman is to be seen. All are ugly and of the lowest class. Here and at Zalamea the people have suffered from the French, but not so much as those of other places we passed through.

Nothing particular to be seen here. The inside of the church is handsome but their manner of ornamenting their places of worship is too gaudy and frivolous. Images of the Virgin Mary in full size are placed in temples and dressed like dolls.

September 4

No orders for marching, which we know not how to account for unless Gen Hill is waiting for Lord Wellington's further directions.

A Spanish Sergeant, deserter from the French army, came in today and gave information that Soult is retiring in the greatest haste, abandoning his sick, destroying most of his carriages and marching for Valencia. His army, very sickly and much dispersed. If half this is true it is enough. The Spaniards positively assure us that our English force is in Cordoba - if so it must be Col Skerret's, who may have followed the rear of Soult's army.

They say also that the siege of Cadiz is certainly raised and that Gen Maitland has defeated the French at Valencia with his army which he took from Sicily. Supposing all this is true, the general opinion in this place is that Soult will be so completely trapped that he must surrender at discretion in a short time.

September 5

A report was prevalent this day that Lord Wellington is within 20 leagues from us. If so, and we march to meet him we may form a junction in 3 days. Things look well and we shall soon want employment if they succeed as their prospects give reason to hope.

As yet no orders for marching and we remain rather crowded. The French levied contributions on this village as on all others, and the mistress of the house in which Maxwell and myself are, tells us that because she refused to pay her share, they tied her hands behind her and laid her on her bed until she consented.

Col Bunbury[4] of the Buffs called on us and invited us to dine with him this afternoon. We went and in the evening Col Byng's Brigade Major called to inform Maxwell that we are to march tomorrow morning at any hour Maxwell thinks proper, for Don Benito. Col Byng's Brigade is to march for that place at 2, and therefore it is fixed we are to move at half past one o'clock. The distance 5 leagues and the direction to the Northward. Headquarters will move in the morning also from Castuera to Villanueva de la Serena, 1 league East of Don Benito.

September 6

At half past one, according to orders, we marched. The first part of the road good, but about half way it was so bad and rocky that being dark it was impossible to choose the best part of it, and one of the ammunition wagons upset. Luckily no damage was done except to the perch which was split near the eye bolt. The country open till within 6 miles of this place when we passed between two hills or mountains, the top of one covered by a cloud. After this a most delightful view presented itself - an extensive plain of marsh, 2 leagues square, bounded on the North by the Guadiana river and the mountains on the other side; in other directions by hills forming a continued chain.

To the North West is seen the town and castle of Medellin built on this side of the Guadiana, the former on the plain, the latter on a very high rock, looking over the town and commanding it. To the Northward we saw the tower of the church of Benito and to the Eastward on a hill to our right is an old castle in ruins. To the North East is also seen the tower of the church of Villanueva.

The river is not seen, but previous to my being informed of its being near, or that we were likely to see it, I remember that I thought

47

there must be a river at the base of the mountains in our front from the sudden change in the face of the country. These mountains extend as far as the eye can reach and have a grand appearance particularly at sunrise - the time we saw them first. The clouds of night and the heavy fogs were dispersing and every succeeding minute opening to our view some hill still higher than the one we had been just admiring. The ground we were passing over is as level as a bowling green, and on each side of the road are melon gardens, covering I suppose a space of 200 acres.

The poor people subsist on the fruit in great measure when in season and it must be very wholesome. The men relish it very much and it requires the greatest attention on the part of the officers to see the gardens are not stripped; for if a column of six or seven thousand passes and every man is allowed to help himself, farewell to the poor labourer's expectation. On our entering the town, the first Brigade,[5] which had been in it for two days, was exercising. It being a public day with the inhabitants, a great many were assembled to see it.

This town, which is said to be the largest in Spanish Estremadura, is not at all striking in appearance. The church and its tower with the several turrets on the body are the only objects worth notice. We arrived at half past eight and found cantonments for the men and quarters for ourselves ready. The horses are under cover also. I have a good billet supplied with water.

This day the members of the new constitution (formed in consequence of a decree by the Cortes some time ago) began to exercise their function and to transact public business, and from the gratifying intelligence received from all quarters the public celebrate it in the most particular manner.[6] High Mass is performing in the church. The houses are to be illuminated and fairs are to be held every day this week. Every Spaniard is dressed in his best and the women seem to vie with each other in adorning themselves.

This does not convey any idea of the wretched state of the country as represented in the English newspapers, but this town has by some means escaped the ravages of the enemy and the houses are in good order. Perhaps this leniency may be attributed to the easy consent of the inhabitants to comply with the demands they everywhere impose. The French will do no mischief when this is the case, but how despicable is that man who will quietly submit to pay a sum perhaps as large as the value of his house merely to insure the safety of it, when at the same time he is giving shelter and assistance to the enemies of his country.

I am glad to observe this has not happened in many towns which I have been in and the French have seldom found anything but the bare walls, unless by their rapid movements they have taken the inhabitants by surprise, or unless by their artful intrigues they have duped them with the idea of being spared from contribution. This has been several times practised with success and perhaps the enemy have been as conciliatory as possible till the eve of the move when they have robbed them of everything and even taken the apparel from their persons: besides breaking their glasses, crockery and everything that did not escape their notice.

September 7

The whole Division still in cantonments and no movements have been made by any part of the troops I believe since we arrived here. Report says that Soult is at Cordoba and has been reinforced by Suchet and that this latter general has been obliged to evacuate Valencia in consequence of his defeat by General Maitland.

The Spaniards say also that Ballesteros [7] has taken the greater part of the army which besieged Cadiz, or at all events that he has intercepted them and cut off their retreat. I fear good news is magnified as usual and that it now comes too quick to be true, though it is well known everything is going on more successfully than the most sanguine could have expected.

Another piece of news is that money is on the road and expected here today, which the army is much in want of, being 5 months in arrears and we of course can get nothing but our rations.

I went this evening to Headquarters, Villanueva, passing through vineyards, melon gardens and fig groves. The grapes have the finest flavour of any I have tasted. The Commissary, Mr Routh had invited all the gentle Spanish families in the place to a Ball and they gave an entertainment beforehand: a bull fight, which I saw by chance. There the animal was tormented by men presenting a handkerchief or piece of cloth, fastened at the end of a pole at his face and he was unable to do any mischief unless a man fell, as a rope was fastened to his horns and held by two men so that he could only run to its extent.

I went to the top of the church for a view of the surrounding country, which is beautiful. The town has suffered a little, particularly a large public building (perhaps a Council Chamber) built by Charles III of Spain, and now a ruin. One street is pretty and contains some excellent houses, one of which is occupied by Sir Rowland Hill. Two regiments of Cavalry [8] are there under General Slade.

September 8

A mail was dispatched for England this morning and one arrived, but the letters were not delivered at this place till the mail was gone. I received two packets from my father and sent him and Mrs Keating each a letter. I have not yet seen the newspapers, but understand Lord Wellington is raised to the title of Marquis Wellington and that the Houses in London were illuminated three nights successively.

By my letters from England I was much distressed by the account of Miss Thompson's death, which was as unexpected as melancholy. She was an ornament of society and by her engaging, unaffected manners gained the admiration of everyone. Other subjects contained in these letters tended to depress my spirits and the only consolation I had was the happiness of knowing my mother was better and that my brother [9] has been successful in the Mediterranean.

Col Bunbury I find sent for me last night to attend a dance he gave to some Spanish ladies, but owing to my ride to Villanueva I lost the chance. This day 9 years ago I obtained my commission and hope the next nine years may pass over with as few troubles, but with more domestic happiness, which has of late been so much interrupted by the death of one most dear to us and other considerations.

September 9

This morning at 5 I rose and at 6 mounted my mule to take a solitary ride for the sake of contemplation and another perusal of yesterday's letters, undisturbed by anyone. I rode to Medellin and the ground between that town and this, 4 miles distant, brought an occurrence to my recollection, which well accorded with my melancholy thoughts. I had been informed that the plain on which the Spanish General Cuesta fought the desperate battle with a Division of the French army [10] 8 years ago was near this place and seeing human skulls, bones etc, convinced me I was on the spot. The Spaniards say 8,000 men fell on that day owing to the fate of it being for some time uncertain, but unfortunately the French turned one of the flanks of the Spanish army and the carnage became dreadful.

It is always the wish of an army after an engagement to have sufficient time to bury their dead, and a flag of truce is generally sent by the vanquished to request permission, which is always granted unless the latter are obliged to retire. But in this case, I believe, the Spaniards retired most rapidly and left their dead on the field. The flesh is soon devoured by birds or dogs, which otherwise would be the cause of fevers in such a climate and at this season. The skulls and bones are scattered in all directions and no perfect skeleton is to be found. Several hundred bodies were thrown into the Guadiana, which was on the left flank of the enemy. I enquired of a Spaniard if he saw the action and he answered, 'Yes, Sir, I saw it all and know that 8,000 were killed' - which he said with as much indifference as if he had been talking of the death of sheep.

I proceeded to Medellin which at the time alluded to above was in possession of the French army, though now in the hands of the Spaniards. The first building which attracted my notice was a large convent, almost in ruins, the roof and most of the walls having been destroyed by the French. The chapel, which bears some marks of having been richly ornamented, is in a sad state. This and the cloisters have been the quarters of some French cavalry at different times. The houses are in a deplorable condition and not more than 12 or 14 I think are inhabited. The chapels and other places of worship were destroyed and only one part of the church remains which is kept locked except during Divine service and therefore I could not see it.

I then went to the castle built on a very high rock of coarse marble mixed with granite, and from its appearance thought it a strong piece of fortification; instead of which it is nothing but a place of retreat and could be maintained a short time only if attacked by an enemy in possession of the hills on the other side of the Guadiana, two of which completely command it within a range of 1,200 yards. But it was built perhaps 200 or 300 years ago, before the invention of artillery and at that time must have been a very strong post. There are two towers, North and South, and a circular building in the body of the castle which has been a chapel. The wall which forms an angle to the eastward encloses a large space - I suppose intended for the inhabitants of the town if obliged to fly to it for shelter or protection. There are no ramparts, therefore guns cannot be placed in any part of the castle. At a distance it has a very grand appearance, especially at close of day, when it seems towering above all around it.

From thence I went to the bridge which is very handsome and light in its appearance, resembling an aqueduct. There are about 22 arches, the centre very wide over which, on the wall, is erected a kind of monument with an inscription in Spanish to commemorate the period in which the bridge was built and its founder's name etc. It was built in the year 1680, but I forget the name. On the left are the ruins of the old bridge which I suppose was destroyed by the force of the current and by the river rising to such a height.

The road on the other side to the left leads to Badajoz and to the right to Trujillo and the North. I rode by the side of the river and passed two corn mills; the latter I entered to see the method of grinding, which I found nearly similar to our own. The building is half an oval, the round part facing the current, the opposite side straight and looking towards the bridge. The windows or holes for admitting light are on that side, as the Guadiana so soon rises that the inhabitants might be surprised in the night by a cold bath if the water could enter. It may happen that no rain falls in the neighourhood and that they are not aware of any up the country, but 24 hours hard rain would cause such a rapid rise of the river as to render it impossible for the people to make their escape till the river had fallen to its usual depth. At the season when rain is expected the mills are deserted and all the machinery which can be taken away is carried to the land habitations.

I forgot to mention that the mills are erected on a bank in the centre of the river and in dry weather are high and dry except where the water is intended to run for the use of the mill. But in the rainy season, although the buildings are about 20 feet above the level of the water, they are almost covered, seldom any part but the roof to be seen.

The people that work the mills therefore follow two kinds of trade: in the summer they are millers and in the winter perhaps bakers or muleteers. There are few rivers which are influenced so much by a fall of rain as the Guadiana owing I suppose to its taking its source from a valley surrounded by hills which, receiving the water from all, must collect such a body as to carry everything before it.

After quitting the river I rode over the ground, which during the desperate battle I have before alluded to, was occupied by the right flank of the Spanish army. Skulls and bones of men and horses were lying in many places but the ground had been much cultivated since that time and the bones have been either buried by the plough or thrown into the river. I observed several round spots where a great many of the dead were buried, but these were the bodies of the French. The distance, by taking this round, was about 3 leagues and I returned quite ready for a second breakfast.

In the evening I rode to Headquarters with Captain Goldfinch of the Engineers and learnt that the musket ball cartridge or small arms ammunition and commissary stores are going on the road to Trujillo, so that we may expect to march that way.

The news of General Maitland having obliged the enemy to evacuate Valencia is credited, but nothing is known relative to Lord Wellington's intentions. He is still at Madrid and it appears no movements have been made by his army lately.

September 10

I found this morning that Frith called last night with an invitation to a Ball at some staff officer's house which was particularly well attended. Information received that Ballesteros has actually taken 2,000 prisoners and two pieces of artillery from Soult in a partial action with some of his troops in Granada, in the capital of which province Soult now is, and Ballesteros six leagues from him. This intelligence is confirmed by a letter from the latter to Sir Rowland Hill.

In the evening Maxwell and myself went over the ground where the battle was fought as I wished to show it to him. We met three Spanish priests; intelligent men, and from them owing to Maxwell's being conversant in their language, we obtained the following account of the melancholy day. ...

The French had been in possession of Medellin (4 leagues hence) and were commanded by Marshal Victor. The Spanish army under Cuesta, amounting to more than 20,000 men, occupied this place. The French advanced their light infantry and cavalry to within a mile of the town, when the Spaniards, already prepared, turned out and formed in line - the right on the Guadiana and the left on the convent three miles from it. The cavalry were on the left and rear of the infantry, and the artillery on the flanks. The enemy advanced in two solid columns, the left towards Medellin to turn the right of the Spanish line, and the right supported by cavalry from the village down the river, to attack the left and strongest flank. The Spanish infantry remained firm, but their cavalry did not support them. [11]

After the inspection I went to the ruins of a large convent and church below the castle but saw nothing except rubbish, the only remains of a very extensive building. In the evening I rode towards Casillos, but as night was fast approaching, and expecting to march tomorrow (from having met near 200 commissary mules on the road to Almusaz) I thought it better to return to my quarters. At the distance I was from the village it appeared to contain no good houses and to have suffered from the French as much as other places.

TRUJILLO

September 14

At 5 this morning we marched for Santa Cruz [de la Sierra], distant 3 leagues and a half by a rough road and rather hilly. About half way we crossed a ravine by a large stone bridge under which the ground has the appearance of being the course of a river, and on enquiring I found that in the rainy season water from the hills on each side collects there and is very deep, covering a space of a quarter of a mile in length and, near the bridge, about 150 yards in width.

On our approach to Don Benito, one of the hills, the highest in view to the Northward of the Guadiana, had been pointed out to me as a landmark for the direction of Trujillo, which is 3 leagues beyond it but in line with its ridge. We were now close to it and a most romantic one it is. Along the ridge on its highest part are several trees and it seems extraordinary that anything can grow there, as nothing is to be seen but masses of granite rock. On its side are trees of all kinds, vineyards, olive groves and through these runs an aqueduct which supplies the village with water.

Some of the Infantry went on to a village a mile distant called Santa Cruz de la Sierra. Our village is Puerto de Santa Cruz and we found good quarters for ourselves, the Portuguese Artillery and Colonel Byng's Brigade of Infantry. Headquarters moved on to Trujillo, 3 leagues in advance. I wrote a short letter to my father in the afternoon and despatched it by the mail which went from Headquarters this evening.

At 6 o'clock I took a Spaniard as a guide and ascended the mountain and though we went the shortest way and made great haste I did not reach the summit till after 7, and then quite exhausted from want of breath. I never was so much deceived as to the height of a place, and when half way to the top it seemed as if I had just commenced the undertaking.

I was highly gratified by the most extensive view I have seen since I was on the Rock of Lisbon. To one direction Trujillo appeared to great advantage; in another several villages or a few houses here and there; opposite to them a ridge of hills and turning about I saw the hills near Don Benito, but the day was almost closed and thinking I should find my way to the plain with difficulty, I began to descend feeling the ground for some time with one foot before I ventured to move the other. On the top I noticed something like a sepulchre, and in two level places on the side of the rock I saw places which one would fancy were hermitages, but they have been made for some kind of animal - perhaps the goats.

The huge masses of rock are very grand and seem ready to fall and crush everything below. The soil being well watered from the several springs is very fertile and everything looks in the most flourishing state. The morning was very wet, attended with thunder and lightning, and the day before and all the time I was out this evening, the lighting was incessant.

I returned to my quarters at half past eight and went to bed rather fatigued but pleased with my walk.

September 15

At 5 this morning we marched for Trujillo, distance 3 leagues, having the town in view nearly the whole way. It stands on a rocky eminence and commands the plain around it. Philaotti [?] appears large but in ruins, as do many of the public buildings, notwithstanding which the place has a fine effect. The approach is by a pretty good road being the main one from Badajoz and Madrid and we gained it near Santa Cruz de la Sierra. This village is built in a plain at the foot of a mountain, but in line with the ridge and is therefore distinguished from Puerto de Santa Cruz by the substitution of the word Sierra. It is a delightful spot. Every house surrounded by trees and gardens or immense pieces of rock which give it a grand and picturesque appearance.

About half a mile from Trujillo we crossed the river Mayasco [Magasca?], which runs over a bed of rocks in that part, by a good stone bridge and then began the gradual ascent to the town. Our [gun] park was formed near the ruins of a convent outside its gateways and our men and horses occupied a large convent and Church near the Grand Place.

The morning was very wet and while we were there, our horses under cover, the rain fell in torrents. One flash of lightning succeeded another, but at this time in particular it was vivid and dangerous and the thunder more grand than any I had heard and so close that a mule was killed very near to us, and being in a narrow street the peal of thunder echoed in all directions and was as loud as the report of an explosion of a magazine.

On our arrival we found that Headquarters had advanced to Torrecillas [de la Tiesa] attended by all the Cavalry and that the Infantry were to march there tomorrow and the whole to ford the Tagus on the following day if it is passable, but I dare say it is impossible that it can be after the fall of rain we have had the last three days. The pontoon train is expected here tomorrow but I am surprised we have to wait for it as it should have been ordered up to Don Benito and been ready to move with us. I think the Bridge Master will have difficulty in laying the pontoons and when laid that they may be in danger from the rapidity of the current.

Frith, Maxwell and myself, after the weather had cleared up a little, went up to the castle, now in ruins. Our first object was to see the tomb of Colonel Squires [12] of the Engineers who died here from excessive fatigue in May last. We found it and seeing the stonework with the inscription on it corroborated the account of the noble and generous conduct of the French officers who were here soon after the place was evacuated by our troops. The Alcade [13] told us the story and as it reflects so highly on the honour of our enemies, I must give it.

Colonel Squires was a most meritorious officer and had received his last two advances in rank from his distinguished conduct on several occasions, particularly during the late siege of Badajoz, in consequence of which (and of Lord Wellington's notice in his despatches) he obtained the rank of Lieutenant-Colonel by brevet, but unfortunately died before the letter announcing his promotion reached him.

The high respect every officer felt anxious to pay to his memory induced Colonel Dickson [14] of the Artillery, who was here, to make every exertion to finish the tomb before the British troops had orders to march, which was every hour expected. However he could not complete it and left the large stone which was to be placed over it with the Alcade, with strict injunctions to finish it. A few hours after the French entered the town and the Alcade, fearing he might suffer if detected in doing anything for us, resolved on trusting to the generosity of the French Commander and immediately made him acquainted with all the circumstances.

The officer, whose name I have not been able to learn, not only permitted the Alcade to do as he had been desired, but rendered him every assistance as to money and otherwise to have it completed immediately, with directions that he should be informed when it was so; which being done, he assembled all the French officers and formed a procession and the road to the grave was lined with his men, after which the stone was placed in the most solemn manner. Such conduct is noble and notwithstanding the character given (deservedly) to the French troops, we often hear of the humanity and generosity of some of them to our officers who may be their prisoners. The tomb is plain and the stone bears the following inscription: 'Lieut Col. Squires of the Royal Engineers died 19 May 1812.'

The castle has been very extensive and strong, both from its works and natural position, but it was built long before the invention of artillery and then must have been almost impregnable. In one part is the ruin of a chapel and near that are the ruins of five convents and their chapels, all which have been destroyed by the French. The castle I believe the Spaniards and time have reduced to its present state. It contains some ancient baths, but they are not worth looking at I am told. They are in a part of the castle which is locked up, otherwise I should not have been satisfied without seeing them, and the man in charge of the key was not to be found.

From there I went to the house which belonged to the famous Pizarro. It is large but shows neither taste nor splendour in its structure. His arms emblematical of the military trophies he gained are well carved over the entrance and chalked in black at the head of the staircase. His crest was a tree with two bears climbing and part of the arms described 5 captive kings (whom he had subdued) with chains round their wrists. Another large house which I was informed belonged to him also is by far the handsomest and most commodious, but a Spaniard told me afterwards that it had been the house of a Count now in Madrid.

In the principal Church, which is very old, is the tomb of one of Pizarro's ancestors and in another is that of the great Pizarro. For what reason I don't know, but the French have removed his body some years ago to Madrid, where its remains are now deposited. The latter Church is on a hill near the castle and Pizarro's tomb is on the left-hand side, near the altar. There are no ornaments or any marks by which a stranger could discover the place except his crest. The inscription is hardly legible owing to the interior of the Church having been much damaged and defaced within these few years. It had been modernized and I may say spoilt as the ancient grandeur and magnificence for which it was once noticed is now concealed by a mud-coloured plaster and marked into squares with white lines.

The Church in the Plaza, near the house of Pizarro's family, is very handsome and grand. The dates of some of the tombstones were in the year 1525 etc - a great many in that century but some in the one preceding. The date of the death of that Pizarro which I first alluded to is 1680 I think. The hero died about 70 years earlier. [Pizarro in fact died in 1541].

There are several antiquities worth notice and deserve a better account than I can give of them, being able to form no other opinion than what might occur at first sight, having no one to explain the particulars and being left entirely to judge of them from their present appearance. I am convinced several satisfactory accounts might be obtained.

The town, as I have said, stands on a rocky eminence on the summit of which are the ruins of the castle. Immense rocks are seen in every direction, many serving as the best foundations for the houses. I thought the situation with a little assistance from art might render Trujillo a very strong place; and being in a plain and commanding it on all sides, I wonder it has never been fortified. It certainly has been a town of great note and bears proofs of having contained more public buildings than any other in proportion that I have seen in this country.

September 16

At nine this morning Lifebure's [15] Troop of Horse Artillery arrived and formed their park near ours. The Brigade of Infantry under orders to march for Almaraz still remain, as it has been ascertained that the Tagus is not fordable and they must remain till the bridge is placed and it has not yet even arrived here.

The town is full of troops: three Brigades of Infantry and four of Artillery and though to outward appearance at a mile off one would suppose twice the number of men could find quarters, yet here owing to the ravages of the French, half the houses are in ruins and not habitable. Officers were obliged to double up and Swabey [16] of the Horse Artillery is my companion. He breakfasted with me and we went to explore the castle and the desolated convents.

Finding nothing particular we went to the house which I have said belonged to a convent in Madrid. The Patranie or Head had the day before a great pile of green wood and I remarked at the time that I could not imagine the motive for collecting such a quantity of it, unless as a substitute for smoke balls to smother everyone near it. However this morning the secret was discovered: six brass 6-pounders and two brass 5.5-inch howitzers are found buried under the wood. Whether they were last in possession of the French I could not understand, but at all events it seems the Alcade has been privy to their concealment and did all he could to prevent our having them. He was questioned about these guns as some person had given information that guns were in the town, but in what house he did not know, though he did not doubt the Alcade was acquainted with it. The guns etc were all spiked so I suppose will be given up to the Spaniards.

This circumstance only shows what traitors some of these fellows are, as the very man to whom you naturally look for loyalty and zeal for the welfare of his country, has no such noble sentiments animating his degenerate heart.

The greatest part of this morning had been wet, the afternoon much worse. Therefore we could only go out in the intervals. The pontoon train from Elvas arrived in the evening and will move two leagues. We may now expect to move again in a day or two.

September 17

This morning (after a night of constant lightning, thunder and rain besides wind) the weather was pleasant and the sky clear. In the afternoon cloudy and every appearance of more rain. In the evening I took a ride but saw nothing particular except the continuation of the bed of rock for some distance on each side of the town. The pontoons proceeded early this morning and the Cavalry expect to cross the Tagus the day after tomorrow.

September 18

This morning I went again to see the guns which were discovered two days ago and on particular enquiry was informed that they were some of those which had been mounted on the castle of Miravete. After the affair at Almaraz a short time ago the French spiked the guns on the forts there and also at the castle in the Puerto de Miravete and abandoned them. Some of the Spaniards it seems, wishing to secure the protection of the enemy in case they should return to Trujillo, took and concealed them from us (perhaps as traitors they had no other motives than policy and safety) and had removed their guns from the forts and castle to the house I have mentioned in this town. Some have been much injured by cannon shot and I think can never be rendered serviceable.

THE BRIDGE AT ALMARAZ

September 19

At 5 this morning orders were received for all the troops here to march at 6 for Jaraicejo and its neighbourhood. Headquarters will cross the bridge today and be at Almaraz in the evening. We moved off right in front; Lifebure's Troop and our Brigade in front of the infantry, the two Brigades of Portuguese Artillery in their rear.

The road was excellent and after a league we entered a wood of evergreen trees which continued for 6 or 8 miles, the road leading through it level and good. Near Jaraicejo, which is 4 leagues from Trujillo, we crossed some ravines and rivulets and the country became more hilly. About a mile from Jaraicejo we crossed the river Almonte by a good stone bridge, leading the infantry to Biornicie [?] on the left bank in a very pleasant situation with the river affording excellent water close to their camp.

We moved on and were provided with quarters and good stables. The Brigade horses were in the chapel of a convent having bare walls and roof only and the men were in the rooms and cloisters. This is a miserable place and had hardly a good house in it and many others are in ruins. Therefore the staff of General Chowne's [17] Division and ourselves with the Horse Artillery were the only people in it. The Portuguese artillery passed through, having orders to advance two leagues further so that they may be at the bridge at daybreak.

Three carriages arrived while we travelled here and we found the people in them are on the road from Madrid to Cadiz, the communication being open all the way, which must be a great advantage. They had permission to cross the pontoon bridge at Almaraz and no doubt were the first that did, as it was just laid.

I had a pretty good quarter considering the state of the houses, but the fleas prevented my sleeping. Colonel Waller having received information that 20 horses for our Brigade will be at Abrantes in a few days, we sent off a Corporal and Driver to receive them.

September 20, Sunday

At half past five this morning the Horse Artillery and our Brigade marched for Almaraz, 3.5 leagues distant. The first part of the road was good, through shady woods of oak trees. In the distant view in front we saw the Sierra de Guadalupe and near it the castle of Miravete. After the first league the road was rough and hilly but the country very picturesque. We crossed another branch of the Rio Almonte, which runs into the Tagus, and several other streams by good stone bridges.

I have said that we crossed the course of these streams, but only one is to be seen, the others at this season are dried up and no water is found except in a few hollow places where it must have remained since the last rainy season. This we have found in every day's march and the men get so thirsty and fatigued that they cannot resist the temptation and drink the muddy, putrid water which of course must be very injurious.

We now approached the castle and Maxwell pointed out to me the different situations of General Hill's force previous to their former advance to the attack on the fort commanding the pass [18]... The troops had taken shelter in the wood on each side of the main road and as it was found impracticable for artillery to pass within range of some guns planted in the castle, they remained in bivouac with the cavalry and other troops not required to storm the forts and castle. The latter stands on a very high hill and might be rendered an impregnable post. It is very ancient and was never constructed with an idea of artillery being invented. However the French had placed three or four guns there and some in a temporary work below and nearer the road.

Infantry could pass without annoyance as they could ascend the hills on the other side of the road, but neither artillery nor cavalry could follow and this circumstance renders the possession of the pass of greatest consequence in prosecuting military operations in this part of the Peninsula; particularly as the Tagus cannot be crossed at any point within a great distance either way except here at Almaraz, the roads being impassable for artillery.

The object therefore of General Hill's expedition with 5,000 men of his Corps was to take forts commanding the pass and then to destroy the bridge (which the French had laid across the Tagus), after having become master of Forts Napoleon and Ragusa, situated on two commanding hills on either side of the river.

The result of his attacks on these positions is well known, also that he completely destroyed the whole pontoon train, thereby cutting off the enemy's communications.

After we had reached the summit of the hill where the wood runs, and passing close at the foot of the rocky eminence on which the castle stands, we descended by a long winding road to the valley. A small village is on the right, Romangordo I believe is the name. The houses are in ruins and nothing strikes the eye but the church, which to all appearance remains perfect. The road was level and good for three miles after reaching the valley. It then became hilly and rugged and the country more enclosed. We crossed a stream of delightful clear water within half a mile of the bridge and refreshed ourselves and horses with it.

On our arrival at the bridge, to our astonishment we found the Portuguese artillery had not crossed more than one gun and all the other eleven with their ammunition were still on this side. It was 10 o'clock and we had expected they would have been all out of our way by 7 or 8. Owing to this delay I was able to walk up to Fort Napoleon and never saw works more completely dismantled. Several good brass 12-pounders were lying in the ditch, all spiked, together with shot and shells innumerable, besides a great many human skulls and bones.

It is extraordinary that so strong a fort, small as it is, could have been taken without first making a breach. No artillery could be conveyed there for the reasons I have mentioned. Therefore General Hill's only alternative was to trust entirely to British valour and he had not been disappointed.

The Magazine was blown up but I believe did not occasion any mischief - nor am I certain it was [not?] done by the enemy. The magazine at Fort Ragusa on the opposite side was exploded also. The French had collected a great quantity of wood, cordage, etc., for repairing the old stone bridge in a temporary way and all this was placed or disposed of in the different pontoons and set fire to so that scarce a vestige of them remained.

The old bridge which was destroyed some time ago by the Spaniards in a retreat is about 200 yards higher up the river, and has a very pretty appearance - I mean the remains have. There were two arches: one or two piers are perfect and Lord Wellington has sent all the necessary apparatus to repair the whole in such a manner that it may answer all his purposes without much expense. When the Spaniards built the bridge, they placed a stone over the centre pier with the following inscription, 'Bridge of Almaraz, if you fall you will never rise to the same state you now are, but most likely you will rise again.' In dry weather the Tagus below the bridge is fordable, but the least rain makes it swell rapidly and renders it impassable.

The French pontoon bridge had been there a long while when General Hill advanced to destroy it and I believe our army had crossed it after its retreat from Talavera in 1809. The Bridge Master informed me, as did the officer of Engineers, that British troops had never laid a pontoon bridge before, nor had one ever been placed and that on examining records of campaigns and military operations it will be found that this statement is correct. Therefore the greater credit was due to our Engineers, for this was laid most excellently and no mishap happened. Twenty pontoons were floating and I thought the bridge would have been stronger if more had been used, but in opposition to this, the current was so rapid that if it had met with too great a resistance from a body so closely united, it might have destroyed the whole.

The Portuguese did not cross their two Brigades till past 12, having been 5 hours about it. Then the infantry came up and were ordered to precede the Horse Artillery. After that all the baggage of the Division was ordered to cross, so that the Horse Artillery could not get their carriages etc over till 5. Then our Brigade continued, and that the heaviest and carrying the most ammunition. We crossed the bridge and continued our march to Almaraz, (in an hour and a quarter) where we arrived at 8, the distance from Jaraicejo nearly 4 leagues, Almaraz being about 3 miles from the river.

The valley contains only three habitable houses, but a great many in ruins. The three were of course occupied by the Staff and we encamped or bivouacked in a wood on the other side of the place. An unpleasant circumstance occurred. B...[19] in arrest for being incapable of doing his duty and for improper language to M. and myself. Last Sunday we forded the Guadiana and this one has been employed in crossing the Tagus.

{Part of the text is lost}.

...the Cockneys of London perhaps riding some unfortunate horses for a wager, or boasting of their having been at the top of Shooter's Hill, which they consider as one of the highest in the world. Such are the different parts which are played on the stage of the World. Happiness and misery falling to the lot of thousands at the same moment.

It being a delightful day, I could not help longing for a walk on Beacon Hill at Exmouth, accompanied by those most dear to me.

THE ARMY RETURNS TO TALAVERA

September 21

At half past five this morning the Division split up, by the Brigades going in different directions; ours with the 1st, General Howard's, were ordered to Navalmoral [de la Mata], two leagues and a half distant, and we marched to it by a good level road - part of the way through a wood of oak trees, the rest over a plain - having in front the heights of the long Sierra de Gredos, grandly above the clouds, if any are visible, and for the greater part of the year covered in snow.

I forgot to mention that the Sierra de Guadalupe extends in a line almost parallel to this and that we passed it before we reached the Tagus, the castle of Miravete standing on one of its summits. [20] I believe also that I have not mentioned that the day before we left Trujillo the rain ceased and we have had none since, so that the weather being clear, we saw everything to advantage.

About 2 miles before we reached Navalmoral we came more Northward, having the Sierra de Gredos on our left, distant about 2 leagues or less. Navalmoral is a pretty little town and the French not having been in it for five months, it has recovered its appearance very much and the people are repairing the damage which has been done by them. General Chowne's Headquarters were here. General Hill's at Oropesa, six leagues in advance. Horse Artillery and Portuguese Brigades have left us and are in cantonments in the neighbouring villages.

Maxwell and I dined with Frith and after dinner walked up to the top of a hill for a view, in which we were much gratified. At daybreak or after sunset the Sierra looks wonderful and extends in the direction of Madrid further than we could see.

I had a billet in a wine merchant's house and happening to go into the cellar I was shocked at seeing the way the grapes are pressed. Several baskets of them are thrown into a large tub and a dirty fellow with his feet and legs bare, and actually covered with sores unhealed, was treading them and extracting the juice which we all drink with so much avidity. From thence it runs into another tub and the grapes thus trodden or bruised are put into a kind of press.

If Englishmen were employed and properly superintended, wine might be brought to much greater perfection than these filthy people possibly can. I only wish grapes were natural to the soil and climate of our country, for with the delicious flavour they have, I am convinced that with the improvements which the taste and ingenuity of our people would suggest, wine would become the favourite beverage of ladies as well as men. [21]

We should never see the processes which the different luxuries of life undergo. When we do we are generally disgusted. Let a Prince go into the kitchen and see the means used to please his palate; he will say to himself with a sigh, "My horse is better off than I am."

There was nothing particular in this village and I slept the greater part of the day, having been much fatigued the day before.

September 22

At half past five we marched to {La} Calzada de Oropesa, four leagues. The road excellent, over a continuation of the plain and running parallel with the Sierra. Maxwell went on to Headquarters. Two Brigades of infantry being ordered to this town we were much crowded. In the evening I went to the convent and nunnery but could not gain even a glimpse of its fair inhabitants. Nothing particular in this place, which like Navalmoral has not suffered a great deal from the enemy. It contains a handsome church which a traveller may rely on seeing in every village he visits. This evening I received letters from

George Smyth [22] dated as from Madrid.

September 23

The Division remained in statu quo except the Horse Artillery, who are ordered on to Domingo Perez, 12 leagues in advance towards Madrid. They halted yesterday at Navalmoral and will move from thence this morning. I received a long letter from my sister and mother united, dated Aug 30th.

The men employed in inspecting harness etc. I remained while an attempt was made in the shop of a Spanish blacksmith to repair the axle tree which was broken on the 13th inst., but for want of English coals or a sufficient heat it failed. Since the morning one Brigade of infantry had moved from here to Sagatamento [?], a league to the right of Oropesa, therefore quarters were divided and I obtained a good one.

In the evening Maxwell, having returned, accompanied me to Detroth's house. The master of it is a lawyer, a very intelligent man, and amused Maxwell very much as he speaks the language pretty well. He confirmed the account we had heard of the wood between the town and the Sierra being much infested with wolves and told us that before the war the magistrates of every district paid one (or two) dollars for every wolf's head which the peasants brought in, and the desire of gain inclined these people to go out in large parties and they frequently killed a great many; by which means the number was considerably lessened and those remaining were very timid and seldom dared to attack any person.

Since the revolution in this country almost every man able to bear arms has been obliged to take the field and the wolves are unmolested. In consequence of which they are so bold as to come frequently in large droves from the woods and mountains to the fountain in the centre of the town, drink water and return. A short time ago a woman was attacked and devoured by some of them and no part of her was found except her feet in their shoes, the leather of the latter protecting them. Since her death a Spanish soldier, armed, was attacked and though he killed three of them he was overcome and very little of his body remained.

While with this pleasant family an order arrived for us to march at 6 tomorrow to Torralba [de Oropesa].

September 24

At 6 we marched to Torralba by an excellent level road; the distance two leagues and a half, passing ... on our right, about 2 miles distant and close under the castle and town of Oropesa, from which it is a mile and a half to Torralba. On our arrival we found the Spanish artillery in quarters here and though the village is small, Maxwell and I had good billets.

In the evening we went to Oropesa, a very ancient town containing the ruins of several large buildings. The castle has been very extensive and the works, according to their nature, have been strong and well planned. The town has three or four gates; near one of them is a nunnery which I visited. About 12 of these unfortunate girls came to the grating and were apparently pleased with our visit. Two were very pretty and Maxwell engaged all their attention by his conversation which I could not join in. There is another convent nearer the castle but I had not time to see it. The interior of the place has not suffered much, but most of the houses outside the gates and near them are destroyed.

September 25

The Horse Artillery passed through this morning at 5 o'clock on their march to Domingo Perez. I sat on a Court Martial to try a corporal of Drivers for neglect and acquitted him. After that I rode to the town of Oropesa, but saw nothing particular. On my return three covered carts were drawn up in front of my house and I found they had brought travellers from the kingdom of Navarre who were on their way to Cadiz.

In the evening I went to a wine cellar and laid in a stock of wine, Percival paying 4 dollars and myself 3. The quantity was I think 36 quarts. Orders were received from the Division to move and we are to march tomorrow to Talavera de la Reyna.

September 26

The roads now are so good that I need not give any account of them. At 5 we marched, passing several villages on our left. We at last reached the Eastern point of the Sierra de Gredos, behind which is a large lake said to be unfathomable - several attempts having failed to find its depth. Perhaps a current may have carried on the lead, which has been lowered to a considerable depth and the people led to suppose it unfathomable. I know that although the surface of a lake may be perfectly still, that springs have been discovered to pass through them.

Within about 2 leagues of Talavera de la Reyna, which is 6 leagues from Torralba, the town opened to our view and the approach through vineyards and avenues of trees is beautiful. Twelve spires of churches and the houses interspersed with pine and poplar trees render it quite a picture. On our entering the town, the windows were crowded with women, many very pretty; more so than any I have seen in this country.

Soon after quitting Torralba we passed the boundary of the Province of Estremadura and have now entered New Castile. [23] The boundary line seems to be drawn as if to underline the differences in their towns, their inhabitants, etc. Hitherto except when with Sir John Moore in the North of Spain, I have seen no towns worth notice from the time I have left Lisbon but Elvas, Badajoz and Trujillo. The first of these three for its continuous fortifications and the celebrated Fort la Lippe, the next from its having been so frequently the seat of the war, and the last for its antiquity and being the birthplace of Pizarro and other great men.

In regard to buildings, regularity of streets, beauty of women, superior society, not one of these towns is to be compared with Talavera. 4 years ago it contained more than 1,500 houses, chiefly good ones, but since the revolution 1,000 have been destroyed and the ruins of many remain as proof; others have been repaired and again deserted, so that 500 only are inhabited. The interiors of most of the churches have also been destroyed, but the enemy, shocked I suppose with what they had done, left two of the best. One is very magnificent and the entrance by a gothic arch, very grand.

Near this is the river Tagus, which runs close by the banks or walls of the old ruined castle, and a fine bridge is built over it with 'Petrus Mandote, Archbishop of Toledo built this bridge in the year 1540.' I think these were the words on a stone over the centre arch.

The road on the other side leads towards La Mancha. The name of the town is taken from its having always been a large market for earthenware, and the literal translation is: the Pottery of the Queen, or the Queen's Pottery. There is a large convent here but I had not time to see it. The band of the 71st Regiment played for 2 hours this evening to the Nuns in it, who were delighted, as also with the society of the officers.

There are remains of an old wall which appears to have been built round the town and the gates and arches over the different entrances are kept in repair. The French have occupied this place with few intervals for the last 4 years. We have quarters in the suburbs and very good ones. Received orders very late this evening to march tomorrow.

September 27

At half past five the Brigade marched to Cebolla (or land of onions), distant 4 leagues.

Maxwell and I, with an officer of Engineers, who was engaged in the Battle of Talavera, rode over the ground where it was fought. The direction is to the Northward of the town and the road to it through a grove of olive trees. The part where the action was most general is in a plain with hills on three sides. On one, Lord Wellington and his Staff took their stand; on another, Victor and Joseph Buonaparte. Those on the right were impassable for artillery and cavalry. The bone of contention was the possession of the hill which Lord W. had occupied the night before: the enemy took it, but General Hill soon drove them off with considerable loss on their side and they never regained it.

The ground is covered with human skulls and bones - horses also, besides shot and splinters of shells - and seems so retired that one would imagine that, unwilling to shock the people with the sight of the dreadful carnage, they had chosen it on that account. [24] The case was, Lord Wellington found he must fight Victor, and if he had not formed his troops in the position he did, he might have lost the battle. No one could imagine that such large armies could have engaged there and no man in either had an idea that Lord W. intended to fight, nor could they see any ground fit for it. However he did and made his arrangements in a few minutes.

Having gratified ourselves, we pursued our way to the Cebolla road, which is the finest for the first three miles from Talavera that I ever saw. About one and a half leagues from the battle place we crossed the river Alberche by a wooden, temporary bridge at the eastern end of which is a Tête du Pont. From thence we rode on through vineyards covering several thousand acres of land and thought that the town should change its name to Uva [i.e. grape not onion]. I saw no onions except in a few gardens nearby. Nothing extraordinary in Cebolla or the villages near it, where the rest of the infantry were in cantonments. The 1st Brigade were with us.

A VIEW OF TOLEDO & ARANJUEZ

September 28

At 5 we marched to Gerindote, 4 leagues, passing through two villages. The second was very pretty and I never enjoyed a march more than this day's. The road was through groves of olive trees and quite rural and almost made me forget where I was and that war was on all sides. At one of these villages a most beautiful girl of 16 was ministering her sweet service with the general cry of 'Viva Englisas', and I was quite struck with her. We had been cheered by the people of each of these villages and they seemed gaily dressed as if on purpose to receive us.

Just before we reached Gerindote I observed an old Moorish

fieldwork and the ruins of a castle near a village. In every direction with the assistance of my glass I could see a village or town and the country appeared well cultivated.

Gerindote is a very pretty place and nearby, at a distance of 2 miles is T... [Torrijos?] where General Hill established his Headquarters. Maxwell and I rode there in the evening, but it was too dark to see anything. When General Hill entered the people welcomed him in the most violent manner and everyone was anxious to present him with wine and fruit. He hardly knew what to do and would have willingly dispensed with their civility. My billet at Gerindote was very good; Maxwell's much better, and his hostess sent us some dinners.

September 29

At 5 we marched to Toledo, 4 leagues passing through Rielves, and a league further, about halfway to Toledo, we crossed the Guadarrama river by a fine old bridge and ascended a steep hill on the eastern side, after which the rest of the march was over hilly ground and on our right we reached the last hill, when we were gratified with the sight of the ancient and celebrated city of Toledo and the Tagus winding at its foot.

We had some very hard rain at intervals this morning and the clouds were so heavy as to prevent our having a favourable view in approaching. However the cheering sun appeared just as we began the ascent from the valley (through which the river runs) to the gate, and enabled all the principal people to meet us there; not that they left their houses to see us, but General Hill had arrived but half an hour earlier and everyone had been anxious to welcome him. Therefore while outside they thought it better to look at us too. I did not notice so much beauty as at Talavera, but the genteel people were dressed better.

On our right on reaching the valley I forgot to mention there is a very grand extensive building, quite modern which we supposed might be the Bishop's Palace, but afterwards found it was the manufactory of the celebrated Toledo sword blades. The river, which within 10 yards of the road while descending the hill, winds round the building and leaves the road after some 500 yards and we did not cross it as one would have expected at first sight. It buries itself almost in a bed of massy rocks, running in a deep channel to the eastward of, but close to the late Imperial Palace and Castle, which stand on a rocky hill within the walls of, but a little above the town.[25]

A little before we reached the gate we passed through the remains of an old burying place, or something like one, in an oval shape, having fragments of a wall in ruins lying all round it. From their appearance we supposed this to have been a work of as great antiquity as any to be met with in this place, exclusive of the marble and alabaster monuments which will almost bid defiance to time.

In front of the gateway there are two statues: one of Alphonso, and the other I think of Charles V. Our park was formed between them and the Archbishop's Palace, which is on a hill commanding an extensive view of the plain towards Madrid, and the top of the Royal Palace at Aranjuez is seen from it.

The officers of the Brigade had good quarters near the Palace and the men and horses went to the Castle. The entrance to the town through the gateway I have mentioned is rather bad, the houses being small and old. The prospect is soon enlivened by the fine broad street, well paved, with houses on one side and a parapet wall on the other, looking over the suburbs and the winding of the Tagus which, having almost encircled the town, appears again in the North West valley. From my description one would imagine the river's course was towards Madrid, instead of which it runs by Aranjuez through the two Estremaduras.[26]

On our right in ascending the street is the largest nunnery I ever saw, and the poor creatures were kissing and waving their hands to us and seemed anxious to be liberated from their confinement. The gratings are so close and the bars so large that I could not distinguish their faces, especially as the building stands considerably above the street, and they were in the highest part of it. What a shameful, ridiculous thing it is that under mistaken notions of religion so many poor girls are debarred the only comforts the world can bestow. A few of those men and officers who were left in the hospital at Talavera after the battle, and who of course were taken prisoner, on their recovery were sent to this place. Excepting these, no British troops have been at Toledo since Lord Peterborough's time. Therefore it was natural to expect their curiosity would be great.

Some of the people told us they were all so happy to see us they could think of nothing else and that all the ladies were struck with the persons of some of the English officers. Well they might be I thought, when they are accustomed to see such lean, Don Quixote-like looking fellows as the generality of the Spaniards are. The French have handsome well made men in their armies, as much as the British; but with few exceptions their conduct makes them generally so much feared and despised that both the women and men avoid the sight of them when they can.[27] As a proof, all the pretty women of fortune - or without - that could get conveyance, hurried to Cadiz soon after the Spanish revolution, which accounts for the great proportion of beautiful women in that place, as it has been a refuge for all classes from Madrid and every other large town.

My first visit was to the cathedral, and here I must wait to consider if it is possible to give the least idea of what I saw. Architecture, sculpture, painting, history and all other arts and sciences must have almost surpassed their talents in completing such a work as this. In the history of Spain, which unluckily I have not seen, no doubt there is an attempt to describe this wonderful place. I should like very much to be at Toledo in winter when there must be a cessation of arms - spending an hour every day in contemplating the beauties of the cathedral. I can say no more, I find I am without one word to the purpose and therefore, to change the subject I will go on to the Imperial Palace.

This has little more than its walls standing, the interior being much damaged, as I could perceive through a window which was open. Time would not admit of sending for the door keeper for the purpose of going over the building and therefore I can only add it was worthy of its name. The view very picturesque, particularly on the right looking down on the Tagus, running as I have said between rocks nearly 100 feet above it and so close from top to top that you may throw a stone across. Here is built a bridge, of one arch I think, which adds to the scenery. On the rocks adjoining but below the Palace are several large buildings, and on the other side, but further down the river are several Quintas, or country houses.

This place, once resorted to by the first families in Spain, is now almost deserted. The houses are occupied chiefly by shops and families of reduced fortunes. You see no carriages and the genteel people seldom walk out in the daytime. The only opportunity of seeing them was on our arrival.

The castle is a fine old ruin and has been strong, as have the walls and works round the town. I believe there were three gates, but as we are to march again tomorrow I am much disappointed that I cannot see more of the place and could not gratify my curiosity in many instances.

The Archbishop's present residence, the one outside the town, being converted into an hospital for Spanish troops, is a large handsome building, quite modern. General Hill and part of his Staff were in it. The cathedral is just opposite.

There are several other things to be seen, but my time was so limited that I was obliged reluctantly to go to my quarters. There are several of the guerrillas here: fine well dressed men, and they have here one of their depots and a hospital. They have no fixed uniform, but dress according to fancy.

In the evening the cathedral and most of the houses were illuminated on our arrival, but the people did not shew themselves in the streets as I expected. The sword manufactory was shut up, so that I could neither see the interior of the building nor the machines, much less have an idea of the process of the work, which I much regretted.

September 30

Maxwell, having been informed that money had arrived for the army and that some of it would be paid today, desired me to remain for it. The Brigade marched at half past five for Villamayor, 4 leagues distant and at eight I went to the paymaster to put in our claims, but could not have them answered till four in the afternoon.

In the interval, instead of being able to visit such places as I had not seen the day before, I was obliged to walk about the whole time in search of people with whom I had some business to settle respecting the Brigade. I only managed to look at the Archbishop's Palace, where I saw nothing extraordinary, and to have one more sight of the cathedral. I dined with the Horse Artillery and immediately after went to Percival and obtained some money for Maxwell and myself. From his house I set off to join the Brigade, crossed the Tagus and kept on its bank for a short distance.

The rest of the ride was over a dreary heath and at last I arrived at Villamayor. But instead of finding a house to enter and bed made, I saw the lights of a camp and with difficulty found out our lines. There is not a single house remaining. The whole village in ruins and the General in command of infantry with us, Howard, was encamped also. The night was very cold. I rested about five hours and at five next morning we moved off again.

October 1

At 5 we marched to Aranjuez, 3 miles distant; the latter part of the way was through avenues of shady trees with vineyards, olive groves and gardens stocked with melons and other fruits and several acres of potato fields on each side of the road. Every avenue is composed of different kinds of trees and they are at right angles, which together with the variety of trees - poplar, fir, birch, chestnut, olives, pines and elms - give the approach to the town the most pleasing effect I ever saw.

After having been, as it were, buried in this shady grove for more than an hour and when we least expected it, the Royal Palace appeared before us in all its grandeur. But it was a mere glimpse. When we arrived at its gates the grandeur disappeared and the building tended only to remind us of the sad state of Spain and afforded a true picture of it.

Leaving the Palace on our left, and passing through an archway, we entered a large square, on three sides of which are very handsome buildings, while on the fourth and in line with the Palace, are trees and the river Tagus. In the centre is a very high and handsome statue and fountain, near which we formed our park. Our men were furnished with good quarters in a part of the square and our horses with stabling in the Royal stable yard. The officers have quarters in tolerably good houses in a street near the park and we have found the few people remaining very civil and ready to welcome us.

This is really a melancholy place. The houses are good, the streets broad and regular and everything that could have been done seems to have been to make this worthy a Royal Residence and I have no doubt that ten years ago, or even five, it was the summer resort of the first families in the kingdom. But what sad changes and revolutions have there been! Houses deserted, others destroyed and some inhabited by people dispirited, sickly and suffering the pangs of poverty. Every entrance has been barricaded (by the French) with pallisades having loopholes, every wall built higher and the windows of those houses near the entrances to the Palace have been destroyed and the spaces filled up with bricks cemented in, leaving loopholes only. Ditches were cut, bridges destroyed and every precaution taken to prevent a surprise, such was the fear in which the French troops must have been.

This was Joseph Buonaparte's Headquarters after he fled from Madrid on Lord Wellington's approach. The Royal bridge close to the Palace and crossing the Tagus to the Madrid road was destroyed; so was another further up leading to another road to the capital. The latter has been repaired and the former is to be immediately, under the direction of Captain Goldfinch [28] of the Engineers.

After having a good breakfast I started for Madrid. The road for the first 6 miles as pleasant or more so than the one I have attempted to describe. At about a mile from this town I passed the Palace de Labrador [29] and soon after the temporary bridge I mentioned. A league and a half from thence I arrived at a beautiful bridge which is built across the Jarama river and a league and a half beyond that arrived at the town of Valdemoro, 4 leagues from Madrid; the road excellent. Headquarters were established here.

MADRID INTERLUDE

{During the balance of 1st October Captain Webber had evidently managed to reach Madrid and indeed to leave it temporarily. The diary for this day is carried forward as follows.}

... By this time it was dark and on my return [to Madrid] I had not the satisfaction of seeing the approach to the town, but the lights in the houses were cheery after a long ride. At half past ten I entered the place over the Puente de Toledo - far surpassing any other I have seen.

Being late I was afraid I should have difficulty in finding out my friends in the Horse Artillery, amongst whom I was most anxious to see Smyth; and I had indeed, for to my great surprise I did not meet either an English officer or soldier and the people being regular in their hours were in bed. No one could inform me where any British troops were quartered, and leading my hungry horse, I wandered about the streets in the most forlorn manner for an hour at least, when, despairing of meeting anyone to direct me, I was going in a direct line to get to the outside of the city in hopes of seeing the Horse Artillery park and if not, intending to take shelter under a tree.

However my good fortune threw me in the way of a genteel-looking Spaniard who was returning from a party and I made inquiries as I had of others, none of which could he reply to, but begged as a favour that I would accompany him to his house and accept of a bed there. I did so and was furnished with an excellent supper and every attention was shown me. The house was the residence of a Marquis, but he was not at home. The gentleman who showed me such civility was a man of great respectability; I believe an editor of newspapers.

October 2

At 7 in the morning I arose and when dressed my friend asked me what I preferred for breakfast and, fixing on chocolate, it was brought me in perfection. After this he accompanied me to Smyth's quarters and having been thanked by him and other officers for his attention,

79

we parted. I was quite happy in finding Smyth had recovered his good looks and never saw him in better health. The wound of a cannon shot one would fancy was a mere trifle. I called on Ross [30] and the other officers and found all well. Belson, [31] who was wounded by a dragoon's sabre, is quite well also.

I then walked about town to admire the neatness of the buildings and streets and the many excellent shops in which I procured everything I wanted. We lounged about all the day and dined with the mess at 6, after which we went to the play.

The Opera House and principal theatre is shut up, but the performance we saw was very good and the dances of the Bolero and Fandango excellent; the girl who danced most lovely and engaging. From the theatre which is small but very neat though badly lighted, we went to the Fond, a coffee house, to drink some bottled beer - in this country considered a great luxury. None was to be had, the stock being exhausted, therefore we ordered some punch and forgot our disappointment by the pleasing tunes and simple music proceeding from the clock {?} in the coffee room. In this house every comfort the country can afford is to be obtained by money: good wine, dinners, lodgings, etc.

At 10 o'clock we retired to our quarters which were in the house of a marchioness. The play had continued till half past nine only and I found the people of Madrid are very regular in their hours, contrary to the custom of most large places. Smyth gave me a good bed and I slept well.

October 3

I rose early this morning to buy everything I had forgotten. After breakfast Smyth and I went to the Royal Palace, where he left me as he wished to take his usual lessons in waltzing.

The front of the building is very fine and appears almost new. I entered the yard by a gateway and ascended the staircase to the second floor (on which are the state apartments) by a handsome flight of steps (marble). I must pass several things worth an hour's observation, to get into the magnificent suite of apartments which have been kept for state by Joseph Buonaparte, and since his expulsion from hence occupied by Lord Wellington till his departure for Burgos.

The audience chamber is quite a repository of art and one would imagine the whole treasure of the kingdom had been exhausted there and in the adjoining rooms. The canopy is of silk and gold embroidery with festoons of red satin and gold lapels. The steps of marble covered with red velvet edged with gold lace. The chair of red velvet embroidered all over with gold and gold lapels hanging from the cushion. Four lions with globes under their right paws guarding the steps - all of the most rare and beautiful marble and as large as life. Busts of ancient and celebrated heroes on marble pedestals or different stands around the room, besides statues of plaister of Paris, emblematical of several of the heathen gods. Paintings by the best masters, almost speaking for themselves, suspended from the walls which were lined with rich embroidered velvet. The floor of marble in mosaic work.

Most of the rooms, taken even singly, display more taste than I ever saw in any other part of the world. Although neither Spain nor Portugal are supposed to possess good masters, yet in the paintings, divans, furniture and decoration here, the best and most able artists in the world must have contributed their aid.

It is useless for me to proceed further on this subject than merely to mention one small room in which nothing but china is to be seen except for window curtains of silk, doors of mahogany and floors of porcelaine [?]. The ceiling, walls, chandeliers and ornaments for the mantel-piece are all of china, and a thousand different figures are formed on the walls and ceiling. The next room is an enviable one in a warm climate: a bed of red silk edged with gold and by the side a bath of one solid piece of marble with a pipe entering it for supplying water, either warm or cold; what luxury such a one as King Jo had when he wished! The other bedrooms and private apartments are not shown.

I had seen enough to surprise my mind for ever, though I did not feel the slightest wish for a life of such state. My bed on the ground after a long day's march affords me as refreshing sleep as Joseph ever

81

enjoyed, perhaps more so, having an undisturbed conscience. The history of Madrid will of course give a clear account of this Palace taken after a minute inspection of everything. I was only half an hour in it and my time would not admit of more. Thereupon farewell to state and to all its miseries for the present.

On my return to the streets I met Smyth who had been pounding them for a few minutes looking out for me. We took a general view of the buildings, which are good, several very large and handsome - the general post office for instance and many noblemen's houses. The streets are very broad and well paved and what is more agreeable, very clean though we could not avoid an occasional sniff now and then. The arsenal is large and well supplied, but I was too much hurried to enter the gates and having to return to Aranjuez, I made the rest of my way to Smyth's house for a beef steak and a bottle of good port, which I had at 3 and started at half past four.

We rode round the Retiro, a large space enclosed and containing an immense quantity of military stores etc. It has 4 or 5 redoubts at the several angles. The Prado or public promenade and ride is shady and beautiful and the Calle de Alcala running into it the finest street in Madrid, just below which and in the Prado are two very handsome marble fountains - one the figure of Neptune in his car, surrounded by sea nymphs and the other something like it. Between them and in a direct line is the beautiful entrance to the town from the Burgos road (I think).

I have almost exhausted all my panegyric and far-fetched words in praise of what I have seen, and repeated the words beautiful, excellent, magnificent etc, so often that if I see anything still more deserving of those epithets I shall be quite at a loss and must endeavour to invent some word not yet made use of.

Smyth rode with me to the river which I crossed by a ford, leaving the bridge by which I entered much higher up on my right. Here we parted and I jogged on without any adventure till I again reached this place [Aranjuez] and entered my quarters at half past eleven. The night was very dark and I had great difficulty in finding my way through the wood.

Maxwell was quite prepared to start and I hope he may have more pleasure than I had or possibly could have. The only news I brought is that it is intended to make a breach in the fort in the town of Burgos by mining it, which when effected, the Guards are to enter and endeavour to carry everything before them. Two attempts to enter have been already made and failed with the loss of 45 officers and 700 men, killed and wounded; amongst the former Captain Williams of the Engineers, one of my contemporaries at the Academy. Dansey [32] another, but of the Artillery.

Further Junketings
Aranjuez & Madrid

October 4

At 7 this morning Maxwell left for Madrid and at half past the troops here paraded for divine service. In the afternoon I wrote to my mother and the letter went off at 6 for Lisbon, about which time Major Waddell and another officer of the 39th, friends of Maxwell's, begged me to give them shelter for the night, being on their way to Madrid. I did so though it was merely shelter as I have no bedding, only two blankets.

October 5

Nothing particular occurred today. I took a ride through the wood by the side of the river which was shady and pleasant. In the evening Trotter [33] returned from Madrid after his mare died.

October 6

This morning I held a Court of Enquiry by Maxwell's order to investigate the complaints preferred against the acting Paymaster

Sergeant, Corporal Hind for over-charging the men for soap, shoes, etc, which were in a great measure proved. After that I went to the Royal Palace which is a very extensive and handsome building and some of the apartments are well furnished and have a good selection of pictures, but it is not to be compared with that at Madrid.

The gardens are pleasant and well stocked with fruit, but everything is neglected. The entrance from the avenue to the Palace is through a double row of statues of marble well finished. On the left is the Tagus which winds very prettily and opposite one of the principal rooms there is a waterfall, but not above 12 feet. Higher up is a weir, over which the water runs very rapidly and has a good effect. To the right is the road from Toledo into the town, and that to Madrid turns to the left close to the Palace gates, just above the weir.

The beautiful bridge which crossed the river in that part was destroyed by the French some time ago and the wooden one since constructed by them was also destroyed in August last when Joseph returned from Madrid; so that to cross the Tagus you must go higher about a mile, where another handsome bridge was destroyed, but one of wood still remains and is strong enough for artillery. A bridge near the Palace, where the stone one was, is to be made immediately and Captain Goldfinch of the Engineers is to superintend the construction of it; but his task is by no means enviable as he has no men of his own Corps of Artificers [34] and is obliged to depend on the resources of this almost deserted town for workmen, tools and materials. A fatigue party is to be sent him from the garrison every day, but they can act only according to directions, without knowing anything about the matter.

To return to the Palace, in recesses of the pleasure or flower garden wall, which is close to the doors of it, are busts of ancient heroes such as Julius Caesar, Mark Antony etc. Many have been defaced and damaged by the French. Those perfect are great ornaments. The steps leading to the state apartments, which are on the second floor, are of stone and the walls of the same, so that there is nothing to admire except the spacious gallery for receiving company. From there the doors open to the second apartment. The paintings are well done but as I said before, they are not to be compared with those I saw the other day, indeed they are of a different style.

This place is well calculated for a summer residence and a Royal retreat from the noise and bustle of the capital, such as it was intended for, and as such is sufficiently magnificent. Had I not seen the Palace in Madrid, all the praise I could have bestowed would have been given to this, though many houses in England far surpass it in most respects.

The chief cause of the partiality for Aranjuez is from its being a good distance from Madrid, the country delightful and wooded, with rides and walks for 4 or 5 miles on the banks of the river on each side through avenues of shady trees of every kind. And if air is required, by going at a right angle from the river, it may be had in 10 minutes as the country in that direction is open.

The roads are excellent, better than any in England, except those immediately in the vicinity of London, which are too often in the extremes; but those here would of course be the same and worse if the good old Brown Street carts of London were continually ploughing them, besides the innumerable coaches, carriages (with and without names) which are for ever passing there. Here everything is still and quiet and the place is buried in melancholy solitude or rather has been, for there was little gaiety while Joseph was on the throne except what he obliged the people to enter into for the sake of appearances. Intercourse with the neighbouring towns was at an end. Contributions so frequently levied obliged the people to set aside their carriages and to deny themselves those comforts they had so long been accustomed to.

Even now it would be the same in regard to this place if we were not in it, for when Jo. Buonaparte left Madrid he seized every mule to bring off his artillery, baggage, treasure and plunder and scarce a carriage is seen moving here. The only objects we see on the roads are commissary mules with provisions for the army, with the carts of that department also, besides officers, soldiers and followers.

The very cause which I have mentioned as making this such an enviable summer residence has its effects in a different way in the wet season and in winter. The ground is flat all round the town except in one part where the hills exclude the only fresh and pure air, which would benefit the situation. The vapours from the river, the damp air passing through trees, which continue wet a long while after rain, and the moisture from the ground under the trees, contribute to render this a very unhealthy place and we are already experiencing its distressing effects. The men are getting sickly and those who were sick on their arrival are worse.

Otherwise it would be a well chosen town for a halt as the palisades, which the French had placed in every part whence a man could pass, made good fences. The houses are large and well calculated for barracks and have more the appearance of them than of private houses. There is plenty of water and the gardens are well stocked with all kinds of vegetables. I never saw a town more completely barricaded and every way or entrance to it was fortified by mud walls or stakes with loopholes. Every house near the streets most exposed was converted into a place of arms. The windows looking to the country were blocked up by stones or a kind of cement with 4 or 5 loopholes in each.

The first thing necessary was to destroy everything that could be of use towards defending the place in future. The Spaniards and British troops were employed constantly in removing the palisades. Those not required for the use of the bridge were carried away for taxes.

From the regularity and superior style of all the buildings in Aranjuez, it appears that when it was fixed on for a Royal residence, no house but of a certain class was allowed to be built, for not a bad one is to be seen and however poor the inhabitants might have been, their houses gave no indication of their poverty.

From the hills behind the town the view is delightful and the whole seems as a Palace or a continuation of public buildings depending on it. The streets are very broad, regular and at right angles. The whole has a singular, though from the hills I mentioned, a very pleasing appearance. The Royal Gardens, the immense range of wood extending along each side of the river for 6 or 8 miles, the serpentine course of the Tagus, its junction with the Jarama a little below the town and the Puente del Argo [probably Puente Largo is meant] across the latter river about 6 miles off, render it quite a beautiful landscape and I

86

regretted very much my inability to draw it.

After this I went to the Palace de Labrador, abreast of the town, higher up the river and on its banks. The building is small but the apartments are fitted up in a style of magnificence and taste, though peculiar, that cannot be surpassed. The staircase walls are of marble, the steps of mahogany and the pillars supporting the upper part of it of marble admirably cut. Every room is lined with embroidered silk, some with gold, others with silver embroidery. There are no paintings except on the ceilings and they are in a rough way. All the floors are of marble of various kinds, except two which are of porcelain. One room is lined with marble and stone in imitation of it and has some excellent and well formed statues.

I cannot give this rural spot half the commendation it deserves. It seems exactly calculated for love and happiness. Having made a tour of the town and its neighbourhood, I returned to dinner.

October 7

This day Whinyates [35] and Brereton [36] paid me a visit and went to the two Palaces with me and remained the night in my quarters.

October 8

W and B left me and Ambrose [37] arrived on his way to Madrid. Nothing particular occurred. I took a ride into the country by the banks of the Tagus. Heard from Smyth that everything was taken at Burgos but the castle, which was likely to hold out. The remains of Marmont's army is behind the Ebro and keeps up a regular communication by telegraph [38] with the garrison of Burgos.

October 9 & 10

No occurrences worth notice.

October 11

At 10 o'clock this morning we had divine service. The Portuguese Artillery arrived and remained the day. It being supposed that Soult is advancing, General Hill is concentrating his force.

October 12

Information received that Soult has moved more to his right and not in advance. Colonel Tulloh [39] with his two Brigades of Artillery was sent this morning across the Tagus by the Puente de la Reyna to a village a little on the left of the Madrid road.

October 13

Maxwell returned from Madrid after 9 days absence. Immediately after he held a Court Martial to try a Corporal Fowcather of the Artillery Drivers. My presence being necessary I remained and at 4 went off to Madrid. The night being dark and my servant not having made his appearance with the mule and my clothes, I supposed he had lost his way in the wood. Therefore I passed the night in a Posada at Valdemoro and expected he would arrive before daylight.

October 14

At 8, my servant not having found me, I went on to Madrid and in the afternoon met him. I dined with Smyth and the officers of the Horse Artillery and in the evening went to the Ball. No news from Burgos, except that the enemy had made a sortie and had been driven in with loss of 30 men in killed and wounded. We suffered also and amongst the officers killed was Major Cocks [40] of the 15th Dragoons, whose death has occasioned universal regret throughout the army and will be felt by the Service at large.

October 15

Having had a good night's rest in a bed at the Angel Coffee house I breakfasted with Smyth and afterwards went to buy a few things for Maxwell and myself. We had thought of more wants, and it seems the longer we remain near this place there will be no end of them, till we experience the worst of all: the want of money.

In the afternoon I went to the Casa del Campo or Royal Country Residence, about a mile from the Royal Palace. This was the favourite abode of King Joseph and here he had all his private entertainments. The house is fitted up in a very delightful style and is well calculated for the comforts he desired from it. In the garden is a remarkably fine statue in bronze, larger than life, of Philip II. The paintings in the house are by some of the best masters and are well selected. The pleasure grounds and different small houses in this enclosure - all residences for the royal family of Spain as at first intended - are beautiful and laid out with the greatest taste.

In twenty years hence, if the trees which have only been planted about 4 years, are properly managed and allowed to grow, it will be a most enchanting spot. The river Manzanares divides it from Madrid and when the city is hid from the eye by the trees, you may fancy yourself in a retired spot fifty miles from the capital.

I dined with the Horse Artillery [41] and went afterwards with them, including Whinyates and Brereton who were visitors also, first to a coffee house to have some beer, which was very refreshing and as good as ale, then to the Prince's theatre, where we were well entertained with a good comedy and farce and the Bolero and Fandango dances.

From thence at half past nine we repaired to the Ball, where I summoned resolution enough to dance. Luckily there was a crowd and my awkward manner of waltzing was unperceived except by my partner and she thought I was careless but not incapable of dancing properly.

October 16

This day I went to the Museum, the Plaza, Wistellina [?], the armoury and the Retiro. The three former afforded so much satisfaction that I could not half gratify my curiosity and as the day was far advanced I was obliged to leave them in a hurry, but was determined on seeing all.

We received in the evening the melancholy intelligence of the death of Colonel Duncan [42] of the Artillery, who was blown up by an explosion of the magazine at Seville. Captains Cairns [43] and Cator [44] were much wounded by the same accident. Everyone in the Regiment must sincerely lament the loss of Colonel Duncan, for he was an excellent officer and one who always upheld the character of the Corps and assisted the right of its officers whenever it may have been disputed. A man of great independence of spirit, a noble and brave mind. In my opinion his loss to us is almost irreparable, at least for the present.

October 17

I went this morning again to the Museum and spent 4 hours in admiring the wonders of nature of which there were comparatively few, but those I saw I suppose cannot be equalled. In one room was the skeleton of a Mammot (I think is its name) which was found 40 feet below the surface of the earth a few years ago and, though an antediluvian wonder, in a perfect state. The bones are certainly much impaired by time but not one is lost and they are supported by iron rods. I recollect reading the account of the skeleton when it was discovered. There is one of an elephant in the next room which is nearly the same length and height, but the bones are not one fourth the size. The feet of the Mammot are very extraordinary.

In the Museo del Artilleria are models of all the fortified towns in Spain. That of Cadiz is so well and so accurately done that an officer in the room, who had been there, pointed out the house in which he had lived and those of friends he visited there. The models of the fortifications of every kind are so good that an officer of Artillery or Engineers might here make himself better acquainted with the principles of this useful branch of his profession than by a lifelong study with the assistance of books alone. The models convey a better idea of the nature of fortifications than the thing itself, for in visiting the works of a town, unless looking from a tower commanding a view of the whole, it is impossible to have such a comprehensive view as these give. In the armoury there is little worth notice. One long room contains a great many suits and arms of every kind, ancient and modern.

November 3

Owing to different circumstances I have neglected to continue this journal and must now trust to my memory and be more brief.

{Editor's note. The retrospective entries up to and including that of the 2nd November follow below.}

October 17 (Continued)

In the Retiro, which is a building in a large space of ground fortified by field works, are several good guns, carriages and ambulances and 4 boxes of every description necessary for the equipment of a large army; it was the arsenal of the French Corps under Joseph Buonaparte. Fortunately they did no damage before they quitted Madrid, nor had they time, as the 2,000 men left to protect it did not expect to find it necessary so soon to capitulate, and every article therefore fell into our hands in good order and our Brigades of Artillery and many departments of the army have benefited by it.

October 18, Sunday

Reports were very prevalent that the Light, 3rd and 4th Divisions in Madrid and Valdemoro are to move on Tuesday next in consequence of Soult's advance from Valencia with a large force.

I went to some of the Churches but saw nothing in the style of the Cathedral at Toledo. In the evening I walked for sometime on the Prado and saw a quiet assembly of beauty and elegance, besides a crowd of people of all ranks. The weather was delightful and though I am fond of the beauties of nature and art, this sight afforded me more satisfaction than any I have had since I left England, as it almost resembled it. I almost fancied myself in the Park of St James' or Hyde Park Terrace. Everyone seemed in high spirits and the band of a British Regiment tended to raise them higher. I actually regretted when the night deprived me of the pleasure and obliged the people to disperse.

I dined with the family of the house in which I was billeted and spent an agreeable evening. I forgot to mention that on the 14th, the day I came here, it was Ferdinand's [45] birthday, but there was no particular demonstration of joy or anything to inform a stranger of its being a day of note, except the ringing of the bells.[46] On the following day I procured a billet in the house of a merchant of great respectability, whose family, consisting of a wife and two daughters, paid me every attention.

October 19

This day being very wet I saw little and passed it in conversation with my friend Smyth. In the evening I went to a Ball and the play. Information received that Soult had moved to his right, his object appearing to be a movement towards Saragossa for the purpose of forming a junction with the remains of Marmont's army, or a retirement behind the Ebro. Expect to continue here a few days.

October 20

Having purchased every necessary article and seen what was most remarkable, I left Madrid at 4 this afternoon with a great deal of reluctance and still more from having parted with a family from whom I had received great kindness, and returned to Aranjuez. On my arrival I heard that a picquet of the 13th Dragoons had surprised one of the enemy consisting of an officer and 48 men near Ocaña, and taken them prisoners. Nothing had occurred in my absence except the death of two men in the Brigade.

October 21

This morning we heard that Soult had again changed his course and expected to be quiet. However in the evening we were informed that the Light and 3rd Divisions had marched from Madrid at very short notice and the 4th also at the same time from Valdemoro. Of course we concluded that Soult intended to annoy us.

An officer of the 13th Dragoons came in and brought intelligence of that Regiment having taken 70 men and 2 officers in an affair with some squadrons of French cavalry in the morning. The Spaniards were advancing in greater force but were repulsed and driven back to form in the rear of the 13th. This Regiment immediately charged and succeeded in the manner mentioned with scarcely any loss.

The bridge near the Palace had been completed in three or four days before my return from Madrid and I passed over it, saving a distance of nearly a league.

Part Two
The Retreat Past Ciudad Rodrigo

WHILE WELLINGTON with the main Anglo-Portuguese army was unsuccessfully besieging Burgos in early October 1812, Hill's force (some 40,000 strong including Spaniards) remained watching the line of the Tagus from Toledo to Fuentidueña de Tejo. By 21st October the combined forces of King Joseph and Soult were in touch with Hill's cavalry and six days later the British began to withdraw northwards and then westwards to make a junction with Wellington about Alba de Tormes.

By 10th November the united British army of 68,000 lining the river Tormes was faced by the combined French armies of Portugal, the Centre and the South amounting to 90,000 men. Four days later the French attacked and Wellington was forced to withdraw to the Portuguese frontier.

October 22

AT 12 O'CLOCK this day we had orders to march immediately. All the Infantry in advance had fallen back and Soult's advance was certain. The Horse Artillery had joined us also. At 1 we marched to El Cortijo del Rio, 2 miles distant, crossing the Tagus by the Puente de la Reyna, which was ordered to be mined as soon as we were over. Our men and horses were well quartered in Cortijo in the Royal Farm House and Wine Cellar, but the rooms the officers had were without doors or windows and very cold. The bridge was mined this afternoon and left in the same order as before.

October 23

General Howard's and Colonel Byng's Brigade[s] of Infantry passed us at 8 o'clock this morning and we heard that all the Infantry were withdrawn from Aranjuez. The officers of Lifebure's Troop of Horse Artillery dined with us and before we parted orders arrived for us to march the next morning to Villamanrique. We also received the information of Colonel Skerret's Corps [1] being at Toledo. Our advance-guard of Cavalry still at Ocaña, near which a battle was fought some time ago between the French and the Spaniards in which the latter, though in great force, were beaten in less than an hour.[2]

October 24

At 8 this morning we marched for Villamanrique 4.5 leagues in a line parallel to and within 500 yards of the Tagus the greatest part of the way, a very romantic-looking castle on our right about 4 miles from El Cortijo. On our arrival at Villamanrique we found it occupied by a strong foraging party of 500 men of the Spanish Cavalry. In the evening the Alcade called on us and assured us that 10,000 French troops were at Santa Cruz, 8 miles off but on the other side of the river.

October 25

At 8 this morning we marched for Fuentidueña 1.5 leagues and met the General commanding a Corps of Spanish Cavalry and Infantry about 2 miles from it - there to receive General Howard. We had just joined General Howard and his Brigade. About 500 yards from the town all the Cavalry and Infantry (Spaniards) were paraded with colours unfurled to pay us a compliment. We were all supplied with quarters, though much crowded. Two of our guns were, by General Howard's orders, posted on the hill outside the town to protect a Spanish pontoon bridge, which has for some time been placed here. It was for this purpose that the Infantry and our Brigade of Artillery had been sent here.

We heard that the enemy are in great force, particularly in Cavalry, on the other side of the river. General Freyre with 800 Spanish Dragoons is watching their movements but expects to be driven in and to be obliged to fall back on us this evening.

We heard that King Joseph is at Cuenca with his army and two Divisions of Soult's and that the latter's force extends from that place by a chain of posts as far as Ocaña, where his advance-guard of Cavalry are.

Near that place was fought a desperate battle [already noted above] between the French and the Spaniards some time ago in which the former lost 6,000 killed and wounded in two hours. Although Aranjuez is only 2 leagues from it, I never had an opportunity of riding there. The only account I heard of this battle was that the French army of 20,000 men attacked the Spaniards who, notwithstanding they had 40,000, did not stand the charge and the rout became general; only 10,000 made good their retreat in a body, the rest dispersed, threw down their arms and flew to the mountains or some other hiding place.

I wrote to my father and sent the letter by the mail at 3 o'clock. Immediately after I rode by the banks of the river on both sides and examined two fords: one I found practicable for the Artillery. I met

General Howard and he invited me to dine with him. Maxwell and I went and just as we were seating ourselves, General Freyre commanding the Corps of Spanish Cavalry came in, attended by his staff, to inform General Howard that he had been obliged to fall back and cross the river as the enemy's Cavalry had appeared in force.

He said that Soult had 10,000 men in Santa Cruz but that his intentions as to moving up or down the Tagus were not known. General Howard begged him to partake of his dinner, which he did. His staff however left him.

During dinner an officer of the 9th Dragoons and one of the German Hussars arrived with an account of a reconnaissance made by part of the latter's party in which he had seen a strong column of Infantry and other of Cavalry moving on Santa Cruz from some village higher up the river - or perhaps from Tarancon. This intelligence, gained at a great risk by going to the heights near their line of march, was considered of such importance and their Sergeant's vigilance so highly commended that the officers of the Germans determined on reporting the circumstance to Lord Wellington. No doubt now remained that Soult intends opening the Tagus near Aranjuez and threatening or even marching on Madrid.

An hour after the arrival of these two officers, one of the staff came from Villamanrique and informed the General that just before he left that place a squadron of the enemy's Dragoons had attempted to cross the river by a ford there under cover of the darkness of the night and had half reached this side, but were so warmly received by the picket of British Infantry that they retired as quickly as possible. Some were wounded, some taken. He said they had no idea of any troops being in the place and were surprised to find a square formed of British Infantry. Two regiments were there and they turned out with great alacrity and knowing the description of the enemy's force, formed a square as the best manner of resisting a charge of Cavalry.

October 26

This morning we heard that the enemy occupy Santa Cruz with 15,000 men: the addition of 5,000 were by the arrival of the column

I suppose which the Sergeant of Hussars had observed. Several of the enemy's vedettes appeared on the opposite heights. We withdrew the pontoons to our bank and cut the ropes so that our patrols and vedettes were confined to the right bank of the river.

October 27

All the Infantry left Aranjuez this day, crossing the Tagus by the temporary bridge constructed by Captain Goldfinch of the Engineers. The Puente de la Reyna was blown up. The Cavalry only remained to keep the enemy's Cavalry in check.

About 4 this afternoon about 40 French Lancers came from the hills to reconnoitre the fords. 12 came forward, the others remained a mile off. These intrepid fellows kept in the same position, looking at the banks and fords with greatest composure, though exposed to the fire of several men of the line, who dispersed themselves along this side and were taking deliberate aim. Only 3 of the 12 seemed to be wounded and after effecting their purpose all rode off, but promised to come again tomorrow morning.

At 9 orders were received from Headquarters for our leaving this place and in consequence the baggage and sick were sent off directly. We followed at 11, preceded by one Regiment of General Howard's Brigade and had two to protect our rear. We were now retreating not to avoid the enemy, but to meet them in another quarter. Our march was to Chinchon, 5.5 leagues over a very hilly, bad road for the first 2 leagues and afterwards not good.

October 28

At 2 this morning we passed through Belmonte de Tejo, a small village occupied by a regiment of Spanish Cavalry. At half past six through Colmenar de Oreja and 3 miles further on we reached Chinchon. These are two large towns and have some good houses and each two large Churches.

After a march of 9 hours in a cold night we were in hopes that we should have halted. However we were ordered to proceed in half an hour to the Puente del Oreja on the Jarama by Bayoña, 3.5 leagues distant, and expected to find the enemy close to the bridge. We arrived at 5 and at once moved off, crossed the Jarama and went to the heights on the right bank, a little below the bridge. The distance we went by the road was a league, very steep and bad. We once more made our fires and rested ourselves after a march of 40 miles, and 20 hours of the 24 in the performance of it. Thus we had protected the passage of the fords at Fuentidueña on the Tagus and the bridge (which I have mentioned before as handsome) across the Jarama.

The Commissary Engineer, Captain Goldfinch, was mining his bridge when we crossed it and it was defended by strong pickets of Infantry. The wood extending from it along the left bank of the river almost to Aranjuez was occupied by British and Portuguese troops and one Brigade of Portuguese Artillery.

The Cavalry had crossed the Tagus in the morning and attempted to destroy the bridge by the Palace, but did not entirely succeed. Some skirmishing took place beforehand, but of no consequence.

Colonel Skerret's Corps joined this army I understand three days ago and part of it is employed to defend the bridge. He had brought about 4,000 men with him as far as Toledo and from thence they were to take a different route. General Ballesteros is at that place, report says with 12,000 Spaniards.[3] I forgot to mention that General Maitland has been superseded and sent home and his Corps of 15,000 given to the next in command, General Mackenzie. If he had acted according to Lord Wellington's intentions, such a force might have made a great diversion in Valencia and he might have annoyed Suchet's army very much. What has been done I don't know, nor do we know the orders General Maitland had from Lord Wellington.

THE FALL OF MADRID

October 29

At 11 we marched for Valdemoro by Esquivias. All the Infantry except Colonel Skerret's Corps also marched for the same place by the Royal Madrid road. They bivouacked in a ravine near Valdemoro. We put our men and horses into four Posadas outside the town and took possession of some of the deserted houses for ourselves. We were informed that Soult had moved to his left down the Tagus and some said his Headquarters were half way between Aranjuez and Toledo. Two fords were known to be practicable about 2 leagues from the former places and we therefore thought his intention was to cross the river and attack us if a favourable opportunity offered.

Near Valdemoro we fell in with the remounts of Lifebure's Troop and our Brigade's, consisting of 37 fine horses in good condition and a reinforcement of Drivers. My servant had taken advantage of this means of joining the army and reached me in good health after a very long confinement in the hospitals of Abrantes and Elvas.

I forgot to mention that on the 24th Lieutenant Baldock left our Brigade for Lisbon in a melancholy state of derangement. He was sent under the care of Corporal Grant of the Artillery Drivers and every pain and precaution was taken by Maxwell to ensure the safety and comfort of this unfortunate young man. Another melancholy circumstance occurred, which was the loss of Captain Lifebure, an excellent officer who died about the 22nd in Madrid in consequence of illness contracted by excessive fatigue. In him the service has lost a valuable officer and his friends a desirable companion; but above all his wife an affectionate husband. He was only ill ten days, and died in the quarters of Captain Baynes, his brother-in-law. His funeral took place on the 23rd.

October 30

At one this morning we were ordered to turn out immediately, march to a position one mile from the town and take up our ground on the right of the Infantry, who were to be formed in close column and to stand by their arms. Everyone was in hopes that an engagement would have followed at daybreak and all were anxious to fight in defence of the capital. However we marched and continued to march, keeping Pinto a small town on our left and at the distance of 4.5 leagues; Madrid on our right - the rain falling in torrents.

We little thought we should pass Madrid except in the event of a defeat and relied on British valour to overcome every obstacle to preserve that ill-fated city. I never recollect on any occasion (where my family were not concerned), being more melancholy and depressed than in passing by the Puente de Toledo and giving up Madrid to the plunder and wanton cruelty of the enemy. I would willingly have lost a limb in a battle to have saved it, and I know every man felt the same sentiments.

The unfortunate people were so confident of our protection and means of defence, that they would never listen to the possibility of being once more under the French yoke. Therefore their fall was the greater and their sad reverse of fortune so unexpected and they so unprepared for it that every feeling mind must have participated in their grief and distress.

Our only hope was that the rain would continue to fall and swell the rivers so as to make them impassable and that in the meantime Lord Wellington would join with part of the army. Soult is certainly superior in Cavalry and in the plain near Madrid, from that circumstance alone, he might have the advantage, and our object was to fall back on a good position, which could not be found nearer than the heights by Aravaca.

To these we marched 1.5 leagues further and encamped or bivouacked on the ground, as much soaked with rain as our clothes were. We had now marched 6 leagues through incessant rain. All the army had orders to assemble on these hills and troops were constantly arriving.

An affair took place this day near Bana [?] de Madrid between some squadrons of the enemy's Cavalry and two of the 14th Dragoons. The latter completely repulsed them, killing and wounding some and taking two or three prisoners. [4]

All this afternoon we heard fresh accounts of the distracted state of the people in Madrid - some running about the streets to enquire into their real situation, not knowing whom to look to for advice or protection; others in search of carriages and carts and animals for their conveyance; others again destroying their furniture and packing up a few articles for a march, and many leaving the place on foot without any clothes but those on them.

In short, such a picture of distress added to the dismal rainy weather made this quite a day of sorrow. The people were more to be pitied even than when the massacre [5] took place there 4 years ago; so large a British army, having victoriously entered their city and driven everything before them, they thought their privations at an end and that by the spring not a Frenchman would be found in arms on this side of the Ebro. From their being so sanguine the shock was the greater and the disappointment was enough to have shaken the patriotism of the people when such sacrifices were necessary to their cause.

I did not go to Madrid, unwilling to witness such sad scenes, but Maxwell was there and gave me an account of them. Those who had been most conspicuous in attentions to the British army and most forward in rejoicing at their entrance, were obliged to quit it from fear of death. For the French would have been made acquainted with every one and not one would have escaped punishment of some kind.

The Retiro was ordered to be blown up and our Engineers are employed in mining it. All the guns, carriages etc in it are to be destroyed and the explosion is expected to take place tomorrow morning. Soult sent a message by a Spaniard a few days ago to Madrid saying he should dine there on the 1st November, and so I think he will.

Some skirmishing took place this afternoon in the advanced posts with the Cavalry, but of no consequence. In the evening all the 2nd Division of the Infantry and part of the 3rd had assembled near us and we received orders to send our sick and every encumbrance to Aravaca where Headquarters were established, about a mile distant.

Our position was a pretty good one. Our left on the Manzanares and our right on the village of Aravaca, protected by some hills higher than those we were posted on. In front was a deep rivulet and a long ravine and the high ground opposite would have been commanded by our guns. From this order therefore and the assembling of the troops we expected an action would soon take place. The weather was fine and the clouds dispersed, so that there was no appearance of more rain and the rivers were not sufficiently swollen to prevent the enemy's fording them in many places. We had no idea of retreating and were anxiously looking out for Lord Wellington.

October 31

The Light Division joined us this morning and most of the Cavalry attached to the 3rd and 4th. The latter joined us also. Soon after Whinyates' Troop [6] of Horse Artillery came in and from them we learned that a smart skirmish had taken place at the Puente Largo. The enemy's Cavalry supported by 7 pieces of Artillery charged the pickets of the 47th and 87th posted there, but were repulsed with the loss of a few men. Our loss was 100 killed and wounded. The Horse Artillery in bivouac two miles off, hearing the firing, hurried to the bridge and on their appearing the enemy retired immediately.

An attempt was made by the men left on purpose to blow up the bridge which, as I have said, was mined two nights ago, but it failed and very little damage was done.

The 4th Division in retreating from Valdemoro and Pinto lost 500 or 600 men in a disgraceful manner. About 800 broke into a wine cellar and intoxicated themselves to such a degree that very few were able to follow. Many were lying on the ground as if lifeless and became easy victims to the enemy's Cavalry. Our Light troops retook several, but I hear 350 remain prisoners. [7]

All the army except the Light Cavalry had no assembly and we had orders to retreat by the two Royal roads towards Valladolid, both leading to the Guadarrama pass. At 11 we marched, taking the road to the Escurial, all the Infantry of the 2nd Division following up. The

3rd Division went the direct road to the village of Guadarrama. The Light and the 4th with the Cavalry remained to cover our retreat. Colonel Skerret's Corps was divided and their Regiments [8] given to those Brigades most in need of reinforcements. He is to command General Packenham's Brigade. The 6-Pdr Brigade of Artillery which he brought from Cadiz is to be in reserve, but attached to the 2nd Division.

The weather had cleared up and was very pleasant and our spirits were a little cheered by the hope of our meeting Lord Wellington and of his having some grand plan in contemplation to make some amends to the people of Madrid for their distress. I understand the generality of the men think so and are convinced of the necessity of sacrificing their present comforts for better prospects. With all my heart I hope these wishes may be accomplished, for they richly deserve a far better fate.

A great many families passed us on the road; some on foot, some on mules and others more fortunate in cars or carriages. One man passed me and accosted me in English and I followed to enquire where he was going. He replied he knew not, but that he had fled from Madrid to avoid the French, as he detested them and had only time to bring away a change of linen and his English grammar, which he said he was studying with great perseverance. Those troops which were ordered to remain to the last near the Capital received the same kindness from the people as if in prosperity.

In our march to the Escurial, which was 5.5 leagues, we passed two deserted villages and crossed the Guadarrama river by a good stone bridge, afterwards ascending a very long hill. It was quite dark before we reached the Palace. Therefore we could not gain admittance, the people in charge of the door having left it. Our horses were put into some of the Royal stables and ourselves and men lodged in the different buildings near them. The situation of the Palace is very romantic; a glimpse of moonlight added to the grandeur of its appearance at the foot of the mountain, which seemed to hang over it. One would suppose in approaching it by night that it was built in a recess of a rock.

On our arrival we were informed by an officer who had overtaken us that the Retiro was destroyed this morning - the guns, carriages, stores, etc also - but unfortunately in the explosion of the mine, which was placed under the building, two officers of the Ordnance Commissariat[9] were blown up, and not a part of either has been found: both young men.

A Stand At Salamanca

November 1, Sunday

At 8 this morning we were ordered to march, taking the road to Guadarrama in a parallel line with the Sierra. I had a few minutes only to look at the Palace which is a noble building but too crowded and the windows too small to have a fine effect. It is in the form of a gridiron, owing to the determination of Philip II (who built it) in consequence of [St Laurence] having suffered on one. It contains the mausoleum of the kings of Spain and is I am told well worth seeing on that and many other accounts, but that the apartments display neither taste in furniture and ornaments, nor the structure ingenuity or architecture. There are several houses deserted and going to ruin near it and a village about a mile below.

The road was at the base of the mountains, and on our right we had a good view of the extensive plain near Madrid and of the capital itself. The smoke arising from the wood in the Retiro very visible.

After a march of 2 leagues we halted and bivouacked by the banks of the rivulet, close to the miserable village of Guadarrama and near the junction of the two roads from Madrid. That by the Escurial 9 leagues and the direct one, which the 3rd Division and the Spanish Cavalry were ordered to take, only 7 leagues.

Here we heard that a severe skirmish had taken place on the banks of the Douro between the 16th Dragoons and the Hussars and several squadrons of the enemy's Cavalry, in which we had lost a great many men in killed and wounded, besides Colonel Parry [10] of the 16th, taken prisoner. This happened owing to the too great impetuosity of the charge of that Regiment breaking through the enemy's line. They thought they had nearly finished the affair, but the enemy outflanked them and obliged them to retire in confusion across the bridge. They passed the Germans; trusting to them till they could form and rally. However the Germans hadn't formed themselves and the enemy by this bad management gained some temporary advantage, though they did not follow it up.

About this time another skirmish took place in another quarter, in which the Artillery were engaged and a Colonel Robe [11] received so severe a wound in his leg that he expects to lose it.

November 2

At half past six marched and ascended the Sierra de Guadarrama, which is part of the Estrella, and came through the Guadarrama Pass, the only one except that of Navacerrada for Artillery or Cavalry. The hill is very long and steep and like those in Galicia, easily defended by a small force. On the top is a monument to the memory of Ferdinand VI with an inscription not very legible, and my time (being on the march) would not permit of my attempting to decipher it.

We then descended into a fine extensive valley, the hills on our left skirted with thick woods of pine and other trees. At the bottom of the hill, 3 leagues from Guadarrama, we passed the village of [El] Espinar where the General has established his Headquarters for this night. The army under the late Sir John Moore, or rather a Division under Sir John Hope, 4 years ago retreated by the same pass over the Sierra, having been within a league from Madrid.

We passed on to Villacastin, 2 leagues further and bivouacked half a mile from it on the other side, on ground without a tree; so it was last night, and no wood to be had without sending a great distance.

November 3

We marched at half past six for Blascosancho, 4 leagues, the road tolerable but stony; forded the river ... and ascended a steep hill on this side and passed through the village of Lavagos, quite deserted and almost in ruins. Blascosancho is a town but of no consequence. We bivouacked in a wood half a mile beyond it and had to send there for wood and water. In this day's march at a distance we saw on our right the celebrated town of Segovia, where there is an University and Military Academy, in high situation. We were about six or seven leagues off.

November 4

From Blascosancho we marched at half past six to Narros de Saldueña and bivouacked in a wood, passing through Villanueva de Gomez and by several villas or houses with roofs off and quite deserted. I forgot to mention that our route was changed yesterday on the march - we were going on the high road to Valladolid, but after passing the bridge of the Voltoya river we turned off to our left for Salamanca.

Our march this day was only 3.5 leagues. Some skirmishing took place and by the stupidity of an escort, several mules laden with provisions fell into the hand of the enemy. No variety in the appearance of the country - hills and vales in succession, but only gradual elevations of ground and not perceptible in the distance.

November 5

At half past six we moved off our ground, but soon halted to let the baggage pass, as the enemy were very near. Two thousand Cavalry were all last night one league only from Sir Rowland Hill's Head-quarters. After some time we moved on again. but only reached the village of Fontiveros, 1 league from the last bivouac. Here all the army except the Cavalry assembled, consisting of the 2nd, 3rd and 4th Divisions. I forgot to mention that the Light Division were covering our retreat and did not join us. After cooking, the baggage of every description being sent to Peñaranda [de Bracamonte], we marched 1 league further to Muñosancho and bivouacked near it.

November 6

At 7 we marched 2.5 leagues and took up a position on a long hill with the small town of Flores de Avila on our left and Peñaranda about 3 miles in the rear of our right flank, which was protected by our Cavalry and Horse Artillery. We were on the right of the Infantry, on good ground with a deep rivulet running at the bottom of the hill between us and the Cavalry. The Light Division were near Flores, the 3rd and 4th in the centre and the 2nd on the right. The Light Cavalry and German Hussars were watching the enemy who, it was reported, had their advanced guard of 8,000 men 2 leagues from us. We remained on the alert all day and night, but they did not advance and our object was to make a stand only, to secure our supplies.

November 7

Everything being as it should be, we moved off again at half past 5 on the road to Peñaranda, passing a village the name of which I do not recollect. Peñaranda is rather a large town and I dare say formerly was of some consequence.

We marched on, crossing two small rivers by fords and at last reached the town of Alba de Tormes, 5.5 leagues, and took up a position on the opposite side of the river Tormes, which we crossed by a good stone bridge; the Engineers then mined it. This had been a place of some consequence and contains some public buildings, all in ruins except the castle which is going fast.

We bivouacked on the rocks on the left of the river. Not a tree within 2 miles of us and no wood to be had as no one was allowed to re-cross the bridge, the Engineers being employed in constructing works and putting the castle in a state of defence to enable us to make a temporary stand.

Lord Wellington we hear is at Salamanca, 4.5 leagues from us, with part of his army. The Light Division and the greater part of the Cavalry remained on the other side of the river. Our Headquarters at Alba de Tormes.

November 8, Sunday

At 10 this morning, after a night of hard wind and rain, every man well soaked, we marched and had just a glimpse of the Cathedral of

Salamanca and the two hills [12] in possession of the British and Spanish armies at the late battle.

We were 2 leagues from our last bivouac when we received orders to return to it. The rain in the morning was heavy, so that we had to return to ground much worse than if we had remained on it. This change was in consequence of the enemy having moved down the river towards Salamanca. The Light Division and Cavalry were ordered towards that place. The 3rd and 4th Divisions followed them and we with Sir Rowland Hill's Corps occupied the heights commanding the bridge and town of Alba de Tormes and the river on each side of it. This evening was as bad as the last. At 9 we received orders from Salamanca to send for some ammunition and anything we wanted. The general report was that Lord Wellington's intentions are to fight on his own ground. The enemy on the other side of the river amount, they say, to 80,000 men - ours to the same, including Spaniards and Portuguese.

November 9

At 10 we marched along the left bank of the river for Machacon, leaving the Portuguese Artillery and Infantry to man the Castle at Alba de Tormes and protect the bridge. Our march through a valley of oak trees was pleasant and short, the distance only 2 leagues and the weather fine.

On our arrival at the village we saw several bodies of the enemy's Cavalry and Infantry on the opposite side of the river. We were ordered to bivouac in an oak wood half a mile from the place - the most comfortable bivouac and the only one deserving the name we have had since we marched from Zafra. A strong body of Cavalry is with us, the rest are employed in reconnoitreing. We this evening sent a great quantity of small arms ammunition to the castle at Alba de Tormes and received very large supplies from the magazine at Salamanca.

November 10

Several bodies of Cavalry were seen moving opposite us this morning. At 3 in the afternoon the enemy invested and cannonaded the castle of Alba and we heard the firing very distinctly; it continued from some time and the enemy moved two strong columns of Infantry on the town but what the result was I have not heard.

Lord Wellington was on the ground which we left yesterday, gave some directions and returned to Salamanca.

The Infantry in this bivouac were ordered to be ready to march but the order was soon countermanded and we all retired to rest, rather annoyed that the enemy had not attacked us, the weather being so fine. Fight we must and I wish nothing to look dismal on such an occasion, and the weather has certainly a great influence on the spirits of people in general.

November 11

At 9 this morning orders to be in readiness to march were received by the troops in this bivouac. All our Cavalry left us for the fords. The enemy in great force are very visible with a glass and we expect something to be done before night. The weather fine and every man impatient.

At 1 o'clock Trotter was ordered with two guns to attach himself to Colonel Ashworth's Brigade of Portuguese Infantry and at 3 they marched to a ford higher up the river. At 4 we heard some firing of artillery, in the direction of Alba de Tormes.

From the heights on this side, Joseph Buonaparte with a numerous suite (nearly 100) and 1,000 cavalry was seen parading near the opposite bank of the river. Two of his staff in a most dashing style forded the river and came some distance from it. Yet the Portuguese picket, through ignorance I suppose, allowed them to return quietly.

In the evening all the Heavy and Portuguese Cavalry, which I forgot to mention went up the river in the morning, joined us - with them Trotter and his two guns.

November 12

Several French Dragoons crossed the river by the ford near Machacon about 10 o'clock this morning and from the enemy's appearing busy we thought a large force would follow. The troops ordered to be ready to march. In the afternoon these orders countermanded and we heard that Joseph Buonaparte had in the morning reviewed the whole French army and immediately set off for Madrid, entrusting the command of it to our old friend Marshal Soult, whose force we understand is about 80,000 men, 9,000 of which are Cavalry. Massena is of course not with them, though it was said he had entered Spain with reinforcements of 15 or 20,000 men.

This reinforcement had joined the remnants of Marmont's army previous to Lord Wellington's leaving Burgos, but is composed chiefly of conscripts and young soldiers and commanded by a man whose name I have not yet heard. The Northern army is supposed to be about 30,000; Soult's about 45,000. Suchet is in Valencia with from 10 to 20,000 men and it is watched by a large force of English and Spanish troops.

The cannonade which was opened on the castle of Alba de Tormes had little effect and the garrison did not return the fire. Orders from Headquarters for all stores and provisions to be removed from thence immediately.

November 13

Nothing particular occurred near our post this day. Cavalry watching the fords as usual.

November 14

At 9 a.m. heard that the enemy had been crossing the river without opposition since daylight. The garrison of Alba de Tormes abandoned it about half past nine, and after crossing the bridge, the mine was sprung and the entire centre of it was completely destroyed.

At 10 we were ordered to march and, the Portuguese Brigade of Infantry (Colonel Ashworth's) preceding us and Colonel Wilson's [3rd Brigade] in our rear, we went to Arapiles and from thence to the left of Lord Wellington's intended position, the distance from our bivouac about 3 leagues, the village of Calvarassa de Ariba in our rear, about 4 miles, and our flanks protected in a great measure by the river Tormes, which forms a semi-circle from Alba to Salamanca.

We halted at the foot of the hill, about 2 miles from the river and

111

from Alba de Tormes and found Lord Wellington and staff were on the hill observing the movements of the enemy, who still continued crossing the fords in large bodies, principally Cavalry. A large force remained in bivouac on the opposite hills.

After remaining on that ground about 2 hours, at 3 o'clock we marched for another part of the position and when near it were ordered to hasten our march to take up ground on the top of the hill where the Horse Artillery (Captain Whinyates' troop) were already posted and had commenced firing. The 2nd Division of Infantry were behind them, formed in column of companies and standing to their arms.

On our reaching the place marked out for our Brigade we had orders to open fire on a large body of French Cavalry in our front and distant about 1,500 yards. Our fire with round-shot and spherical case had great effect and after sustaining considerable loss from a discharge of 55 rounds, they retired in good order. I never saw troops more steady, for although the round-shot made intervals in their ranks, there was not the least appearance of confusion. Lord Wellington and staff were behind some rocks and close to our right-hand gun, noticing the effect of our fire. The guns of the Horse Artillery were of too small a calibre for such a range and ceased firing when we commenced.

We plainly saw a large force of Infantry in a hollow out of range of our guns and it seemed their intention was to have taken the hill we were then on, which would have given them great advantage, and they would in all probability have succeeded had our troops been half an hour later in possessing it.

A very extensive wood lay in the plain and on our left, which was occupied by a Brigade of Infantry under Colonel Byng [2nd Brigade]. This occurred about half past four; an hour afterwards, the day being nearly closed and the enemy quiet behind a village and some hills in front, Lord Wellington left us for Salamanca.

About 8 o'clock we moved to the plain behind our first position, it being more sheltered from the wind, and remained on the alert during the night. I forgot to mention that while we were firing from the hill a great deal of skirmishing took place on our right between our Light Cavalry and that of the enemy who were endeavouring to outflank us.

November 15, Sunday

At half past 3 this morning we heard the firing of some of our advanced pickets and from the reports of the musquetry being so loud, we thought they had been driven in. At half past four we retired about two miles and soon after daybreak took up our ground behind Arapiles, where the Infantry of the 2nd Division were formed in order of battle.

The army began to collect from every direction and each Division took up the position allotted to it. Ours and the 3rd in the centre and immediately behind the two hills (known by the name of the Arapiles) - the Portuguese and Spaniards on our right with the 1st and 7th Divisions, and our left I believe was maintained by the Light, the 5th and the 6th Divisions; the Cavalry and Horse Artillery in advance.

About 7 o'clock Lord W. arrived and ascended one of the hills and with his staff remained some time observing the enemy's movements, which were very uncertain and tending to deceive him. The weather being hazy prevented his seeing them as he wished and he went to another part of the position from which he soon perceived they were endeavouring to turn his right flank. About 9 o'clock he moved that way and accompanied by General Howard's Brigade took up a commanding post and had a tolerable good view of what was going on.

The ground we left was in some places almost covered with skeletons, shells and bones of poor fellows who fell on the 22nd and 23rd July. The dismal appearance of the sky, the heavy rain, the immense body of troops drawn up on the very graves of their comrades and expecting the attack to commence (and so severe a contest as it would have been) rendered the scene truly awful: notwithstanding we all wished for it and hoped to decide the fate of Spain and render Lord Wellington still more deserving of his late elevation in rank.

After waiting anxiously for the approach of the enemy, they appeared in very large force, as if inclined to try our strength in this second position. During this time firing was kept up on their right in an extensive wood to give us an idea that the greater part of their army remained in camp: this is an old trick and Lord W. was not deceived by it and was convinced they were marching in a direction to intercept our retreat on Ciudad Rodrigo.

About 12 o'clock several explosions of ball cartridge magazines and the destruction of several military store houses took place in Salamanca, which was only three miles from us.

Soon afterwards we commenced our retreat, leaving that city on our right, crossed two fords and retired over very heavy country (almost inundated by the incessant rain) to a wood near the village of Barbadillo, 4 leagues from Arapiles.

Retreat To Robleda

November 15 (Cont'd)

It was 8 o'clock in the evening when we reached the bivouac and a miserable one it was, ankle deep in water and the wood so wet we could not make a fire for some time. Headquarters in a village 2 miles further on the road to Ciudad Rodrigo.

Our march and manoeuvres were very harassing this day and the final part of the road was through cornfields which were so soft that the wheels of our gun carriages sank up to the naves in mud. Those men who were weak or sickly were fast dropping in the rear, certain of falling into the hands of the enemy unless we would mount them on our carriages, which feelings of humanity in opposition to a sense of our duty almost tempted us to do as far as we could - but from the numbers of our sick we only brought on three.

Such a quantity of rain had fallen since the morning that brooks became rivers almost impassable and rapid streams appeared where the day before only a furrow was to be seen. We were out from half past three in the morning till eight in the evening and then had to lie down in wet clothes, as I have said, in a swamp.

November 16

Early morning at 6 we marched, baggage in front and soon fell on to the main road leading to Ciudad Rodrigo. We retired to a wood near the village of Matilla [de los Caños del Rio], across a ford commanded from the Salamanca side. We halted at Matilla by Lord Wellington's orders, to take away a large supply of spherical case-shot which had been sent for the use of our Artillery. We were obliged to throw a great many round- and common case-shot away to enable us to pack the former in our ammunition boxes.

We had only left the village half an hour previously and taken up our ground on a hill in the wood, when we perceived the enemy's Cavalry in large force on the hills on the other side of the ford. We were soon ordered out again and went to a part of the wood where we could have opened a fire within 800 yards of some of their advanced squadrons, but unluckily some of our Cavalry were in the way.

After a little skirmishing they approached us in a very bold manner and charged the 92nd Highlanders [13] who were drawn up in front of us. These remained firm as a rock, the front rank had kneeled down ready to give them a volley, but some of the English Cavalry being in the way prevented them. Another party of French Hussars charged Captain Bradley's Company of the 28th, [14] but were obliged to wheel about, exposed to a volley which annoyed them a great deal.

We were ordered to another part of the wood where there was an opening and we had an opportunity of opening fire, first at 1,000 yards and afterwards at 800 yards, which had great effect and prevented the enemy's attempting anything further. This was at about half past four, and at five we returned to our bivouac for the night. We had one man wounded by a rifle ball. This march was 4 leagues.

November 17

At half past three in the morning we were marched for San Muñoz, 4 leagues. We did not go near the village, but crossed a ford higher up and bivouacked on the Ciudad Rodrigo side of a large wood. About 2 o'clock, soon after our arrival on the ground, our guns were ordered to be posted in such a manner as to protect the ford, the enemy showing intentions of crossing it.

However their Cavalry and Artillery moved to one lower down the stream and by their superiority in the latter force obliged our troops to act on the defensive. Almost all our Cavalry had crossed and the Light Division was descending a hill to follow them, skirmishing with the enemy all the way, when Whinyates took part with his Troop of Horse Artillery and kept up a well directed fire with round-shot and now and then common case on their Cavalry, who at times were within 200 yards and endeavouring to keep the ford. He completely kept them in check till they brought (as it is said) nearly 20 pieces of Artillery to the opposite heights, one near the village of Buena Madre, which was masked and commenced firing on Whinyates' guns. They dismounted one, carried away the wheel of another, killed two horses, wounded 2 men and knocked down Lieut Bent [15] and also severely wounded Major Macdonald [16] of the Horse Artillery, who had left his troop to see what others were about.

Many of the Light troops were engaged and the greatest part of our army was drawn up, the enemy having appeared in great force and showed every disposition to bring on a general action, but the ground would not have admitted of it.

The weather was foggy and the rain falling in torrents so that we could not see above a mile from our position. In some parts of the day the fog was so thick as to prevent our seeing even our own guns, and the enemy, taking advantage of this, took General Paget [17], second in command, in a most dashing style. His Division (the first) was drawn up and some French Dragoons [18] were, unperceived by them, concealed in the wood near their ground. General Paget and Staff rode to the front about 200 yards only, when these fellows made a charge and took Sir Edward in spite of the endeavours of his Staff to prevent it.

116

The Infantry attempted to fire, but owing to the rain their powder was wet. A great many prisoners and the baggage of several individuals fell into the hands of the enemy this day, for their Light Cavalry passed our vedettes in several places under cover of the fog. The day ended without anything further and the several Divisions retired to their bivouacs.

November 18

At 5 we retreated to Tenebron and bivouacked in a wood 3 miles from it. The enemy did not press us as much this day, but a good deal of skirmishing took place between our rearguard and their Cavalry. Officers of all Regiments complaining of having lost their baggage, General Chowne's had been missing 4 days; the troops suffering in the extreme from want of provisions, not having had any for 4 or 5 days. The Portuguese Brigade in our Division are said to have been without for 6 or 7 days.

November 19

At 6 we retired to Zamarra by a pass over the Sierra, leaving Ciudad Rodrigo 3 miles on our right. Yesterday's march was 3 leagues, today's about the same. We passed the village and bivouacked in a wood a mile from it. Captain Cator's Brigade of Artillery of 6-Pounders was not able to follow us as his horses were knocked up and quite out of condition owing to their long march from Cadiz and the scarcity of forage they had experienced over the greater part of it. He reported the circumstance to Sir Rowland Hill, who permitted him to march to Ciudad Rodrigo.

November 20

Halted. Sent a letter to Headquarters for my mother. The weather being very bad prevented my looking about the country.

November 21

At 8 am we marched for Robleda, 4.5 leagues over the worst road I ever saw and which I should have pronounced almost impracticable even for Light Artillery. To my great surprise however no accident happened except that of a wheel breaking, which was soon replaced. The road was over beds of rocks and across ravines, at the bottom of each a deep ford, with large rocks at every step a horse took.

We passed the village of Martiago and on our arrival at El Saugo were informed the ford between that and Robleda had risen 3 feet since yesterday so that we knew it was useless to proceed and got our men and horses under shelter as well as we could. We had only marched 3.5 leagues and had been on the road since 8. It was the same hour in the evening when we halted.

November 22

At 4 this afternoon, having ascertained that the ford is passable, we marched to Robleda, one league and were provided with the best sheltering and quarters the village could furnish. Sir Rowland Hill's Headquarters here.

November 23

Halted. Nothing occurred. Orders received for the establishment of hospitals and every arrangement made as for a winter quarter. Therefore we expect to remain here some time.

November 24

Nothing extraordinary. Received a letter from my mother dated October 22nd.

November 25

Another letter from my mother. Answered both and sent my letters off this morning. Reports are prevalent that we shall move in two or three days more to the southward as there is great scarcity of grain in this neighbourhood. The French army have retired and gone into cantonments - some to Salamanca, and King Joseph they say is marching his Corps on Madrid, where it appears a Spanish force under General Medico [19] has been for three weeks. These I suppose will have to walk out on the approach of the King of Spain, unless they are able to maintain the passes over the Sierra de Guadarrama.

We have not been informed how Soult and that part of his army conducted themselves during their short stay at the Capital. Considering himself secure thus far, he did not delay following us and harassing our retreat when he could. We seldom gave them an opportunity while the weather was favourable and we were supplied with provisions and forage, but men, half starved and unable to drag one leg after the other through the heavy swampy ground we had to travel over, fall easy victims to the Cavalry of a pursuing army. Every man on their side on the contrary - sick, lame or wounded - remains safe in their rear and has a better berth even than his effective comrades.

I find our Division alone lost 700 men in the retreat from Salamanca and the average of wounded and missing, besides those dead, may be computed at 3,000. The greatest number of these were Portuguese, who stand fatigue with less spirit than the Spaniards, and the jealousy and hatred which still exist between the two countries in reality, though not in form, are the cause of their suffering more than our troops.

Perhaps in passing a village one might manage to get something - a loaf of bread or some coarse flour, though we only had this good luck in one instance - but the Spaniards, being at home, picked up a great deal on the way. Our men and officers subsisted on acorns, which are not unpleasant when no rations were to be had. The Portuguese were too indolent or despondent. In one Brigade their Commissary was so negligent that for 7 days he did not succeed in providing either bread or spirits for the men and only two days in that time did they get meat, and then without salt.

November 26

I went this day to Fuenteguinaldo across the Agueda by a ford in a deep ravine, the road to which in descending the hill is not practicable for Artillery. The distance to Fuenteguinaldo is only one league and the object of my ride there was in hope of procuring some necessary articles for our table, of which we were in great need and could not meet with here. I found the same scarcity, although we had been assured things of every kind were to be had there. A little bread and some chocolate was the reward of my trouble.

It is a miserable village - houses mere hovels and many in ruins, all in the same style as the other villages we have seen lately and those along the opposite banks of the Agueda, one of which (Frenada), Lord Wellington has chosen for his Headquarters.

The country is well calculated for hunting and several foxes are in the neighbourhood. He and Sir Rowland Hill (each) keep a pack of foxhounds and enjoy the sport very much. I saw Colonel Hartman,[20] commanding the Artillery of the 3rd Division, the Headquarters of which are at Fuenteguinaldo and he said we are likely to move in a day or two.

November 27

Nothing extraordinary this day. In the evening we received orders for marching tomorrow towards Coria where we hear provisions are more plenteous. We cannot be worse off than at present and are happy to try the change.

Part Three
Winter Quarters

Wellington's Anglo-Portuguese army went into winter quarters at the end of the retreat from Burgos and Madrid. The distribution of the force was largely governed by the necessity of finding accommodation for the men and local supplies of forage for the horses.

The entries in Captain Webber's Journal covering this period give an excellent picture of the life of a regimental officer, his difficulties and distractions and his attitude towards the local inhabitants.

BACK INTO PORTUGAL

November 28

At half past seven we marched with General Howard's Brigade of Infantry to Villasrubias, 1 league only. The distance tomorrow will be 4.5 leagues over one of the worst roads for Artillery in the country. The road to Villasrubias is good and we managed to get the greater part of our Brigade under cover. The village does not contain above 50 houses and in it were two regiments of Heavy Dragoons, a troop of Horse Artillery, the Staff of General Slade and Colonel Byng, besides ourselves. A good squeeze, but the weather being cold, the more the merrier. The Infantry bivouacked in a wood.

November 29

At 7 we marched for Perales, 4.5 leagues by the pass of that name over the Sierra de Gata. The road in ascending the hill is not bad but the worst for Artillery I could have conceived and had I been sent to examine it I should have been afraid to say it was passable, lest the carriages should have been all destroyed - which I expected every instant would have been the fate of many. Fortunately no accident happened except to the Forge Cart, the perch of which broke owing to the violent shocks in passing over rocks so immense that now and then the tops of the wheels were on a level with a rock a carriage had but that moment passed. No one unaccustomed to the country would have ventured to ride a mule over such ground, notwithstanding their being the safest of all animals for travelling over mountains.

The morning had been very disagreeable and rainy and when on the top of the Sierra we were enveloped in a cloud or thick mist, unable to see 20 paces from us, which disappeared as if by magic and opened to our view one of the finest landscapes I ever beheld. On each side in the front, mountains were seen for a great distance and between them a wide extended plain, terminated by the Sierra seen rising at right angles from the villages in every direction. On our left, almost buried in the rocks and open only towards us appeared Gata, one of the largest in the neighbourhood; at which is a tolerable market. Its situation is very romantic and above it on a very high rock is an old castle in ruins.

The village of Perales has a very picturesque appearance, but the beauties of nature are soon forgotten by entering it. Two narrow streets with wretched houses afforded us shelter. We found some good wine here, but it was in too great abundance. The soldiers were seen lying about the streets all the afternoon - stupefied or completely drunk.

November 30

At the usual hour we marched to Moraleja, 2 leagues, by a good road. This is rather a good quarter comparatively speaking. Maxwell and I have a good house, the same which the French General Merle had when that army was in cantonments in this part of the country. The outside formed such a contrast with its interior neatness and comforts that no officers of higher rank than ourselves had thought of examining it.

Lt-General Sir William Erskine commanding the 2nd Division of Cavalry has established his Headquarters here. Those of Sir Rowland Hill are in Coria, 2 leagues from hence. Colonel Byng's and Colonel Wilsons's Brigades of Infantry, two regiments of Cavalry, Whinyates' Troop of Horse Artillery and ourselves occupy the place, but part of this force is to move tomorrow.

I wrote a letter to Baldock and one to Major Baynes in his favour.

December 1

Nothing occurred.

December 2

On the road to Coria when I unexpectedly met my friend

Farquharson[1] who had come across the country from Toledo to join the 3rd Regiment of Foot or Buffs. As he was quite a stranger I returned with him although I much wished to see Coria, the Cathedral of which is said to be handsome and the Gothic arch and entrance admirably executed.

There is a song in Spanish very satirical on the wise heads of that place for building a bridge where there is no river and where a bridge was required they cross in a boat. One line of this song is: 'Rio sin puente y puente sin rio'... a river without a bridge and a bridge without a river.

The fact is that the Cathedral was built too near the banks of the river running by Coria, over which there had been a bridge of many years standing. It was discovered that during the wet season the river rose so much and washed the banks away so fast that at last it began to sap the foundation of the Cathedral. To save this building, the work of much expense and labour, they resolved on turning the course of the river, which they did, and from that time to this there has been want of public money or public spirit to build another bridge.

The old one remains and the ground under it, being cultivated, bears no marks of its having ever been a water course: which has given rise to the appellation which the inhabitants bear of 'The fools of Coria'. The traveller is obliged to cross a ferry on his way from that place to Plasencia.

December 3

I went this morning to Gata for wine and anything I could meet with. I bought some wine - very good and cheap, also some bread. In returning, it being dark, I lost my way and having only a Portuguese boy with me, was at a loss what to do. After great perseverance I got on to a track and went in a line towards a light, which at last I reached, having been 5.5 hours and only one league from Gata had I gone the right way; but I was told even the people of the country lose their way at night. Over the mountains the tracks are only goat walks and there are no guides. The road I went in the morning was by Torre [de don Miguel], but nearly half a league further than by Villasbuenas de

Gata, which was the village I reached with so much pleasure. I applied to the Alcade for a guide and reached Moraleja at 3 in the morning.

December 4

At 8 we marched to Zarza la Mayor. The road pretty good but hilly. Want of forage obliges us to go into Portugal, where there has been a great deal saved by Lord Wellington's order. This is a town and the houses, though bad, are clean and perfect; very few have suffered from the ravages of war.

December 5

The distance from Moraleja 5 leagues. We marched at 9 for Ladoeiro in Portugal, 7 leagues, over a very bad and hilly road and heavy owing to a fall of rain last night. Our horses suffered a great deal. We fed twice: once on the road and once in Zibreira and after all were not able to reach Ladoeiro till 11 at night. We crossed the river Erjas which in this part divides Spain from Portugal.

We all lament the necessity of leaving the former country, where we have almost invariably received the greatest kindness; and even in the retreat, though the lower classes might have thought we had abandoned them, they continued to afford us every assistance that their scanty means would admit of. Every cottage in Spain is preferable to most of the houses in this country; their walls are clean and whitewashed, their furniture, poor as it is, is neat and well arranged and when we managed to get a bed it was cleaner and more free from vermin than any I have slept in since I left England. And what these poor unfortunate people offered was always presented with such a good grace, that I shall anxiously wait for our return to them.[2]

In this village, though Portugal has been free from the enemy nearly two years, though the British Government gave £100,000 to the poor in addition to the large subscription raised by the British officers in this army, and though they have seen us drive the French from their doors, yet when I entered my billet I had no mark of civility or welcome shown me and the people, though apparently in good circumstances, would give me nothing but a straw mattress on the dirty floor. All other officers have met with the same reception here this evening. I frightened these ungrateful wretches a little I believe by assuring them that in less than 2 months they will have their old friends the French with them to teach them good manners.

December 6

We marched at 9 for Idanha-a-Nova, 2 leagues, in company with Colonel Tulloh and two Brigades of Portuguese Artillery. The road to the river Ponsul on which the town stands is good: after crossing the bridge the ascent is by a paved road impassable for Artillery unless drawn by men or machinery. The turns are so short and numerous, without any fence on the outer side that it would be dangerous to attempt to try them with horses. We therefore left and parked our guns near the bridge and brought our men and horses up to the town.

We have tolerable good quarters but all are dirty. To compensate for this however, the people are civil and even respectful so that my opinion formed after yesterday's march must be confined at present to the inhospitable Portuguese in the village of Ladoeiro. This is a romantic spot: houses built in a bed of rocks, some of which form a ground floor or perhaps part of a wall, for many of the cottages of the poor. We have a fine view of the extensive plain in front, but to the rear, right and left, nothing but huge masses of rock are to be seen, as if falling on each other.

December 7,8,9 & 10

Nothing extraordinary. The three last days the weather has been very bad and I have not been able to look about the country. The first day I went down to the park and mounting a hill on my return completely knocked me up. I was obliged to halt ten times for want of breath.

December 11

I went to Proença-a-Velha and the different villages in the direction of Penamacor to find what forage could be collected.

December 12

Dined with General Hamilton, who marched in this morning with the 14th Portuguese Infantry on the route to Portalegre.

December 13

Colonel Tulloh received orders to march his two Brigades of Portuguese Artillery to Elvas to refit.

December 14

The Portuguese Artillery marched after having consumed almost the whole depôt of hay which had been collected here for the British Cavalry and Artillery.

December 15

Maxwell received an order to consider himself under arrest by Lord Wellington and to prepare for trial by a General Court Martial, which is to be assembled at Coria to investigate the charges preferred against him, which were for suffering the soldiers under his command to break open the houses containing hay (which had been deposited for the use of the army) in a riotous, tumultuous, disorderly manner, whereby a considerable quantity was wasted and destroyed and for not having given receipts for the hay so taken. The charges were sent also to Colonel Tulloh and Major Gore [3] of the 9th Dragoons and each of the officers was ordered into arrest.

The irregularities complained of are said to have been committed on the 6th inst., the day these troops (the Dragoons and Portuguese Artillery) and ourselves marched in. The 9th Dragoons remained one night only and marched on the 7th for the neighbourhood of Portalegre.

I had arranged everything and had been promised leave to go to Lisbon. The command of the Brigade devolving on me, I was obliged to give up all thoughts of it, and Lieut Trotter having been taken ill makes it still more necessary, no other officer doing duty but myself.

December 19

General Hamilton and the Portuguese Infantry marched for

Portalegre and left us the only troops in the town.

For the last three days I have been to some of the villages in the direction of Castello Branco with a view of finding one more calculated than this place as a cantonment for the Brigade. Our forage nearly exhausted, the nature of the ground so bad for the daily exercise of the horses - makes it advisable to apply for a move. I have written to the Quartermaster General of the Division and fixed on Alcains.

I met a Spanish Commissary, the very man I wished to see, having been informed he had charge of all the Depôts of hay and obtained from him the necessary information as to the quantity contained in them and their relative situation. After this he insisted on my dining with him, and having no reasonable excuse and seeing I should offend him if I did not, I consented.

At his house I met a large party of Portuguese who had also been invited to dine with him. His wife, a pleasing woman, was very polite to me and what with a most excellent dinner to which I had not of late been accustomed, dressed quite in the English style, the attention and hospitality of the Commissary (Don Francisco) and some good singing and music after dinner, in which Madam took part, I passed a very pleasant evening. I was much pressed to stay, but I could not and at 8 left them with my guide to ride 4 leagues in a very dark night. He brought me home quite safe and much satisfied with my trip and reconnaissance.

Sgt Payne of the Artillery Drivers was attacked with fever this day and the Commissary of our Brigade also with a violent fit of ague. The men seem to be getting sickly as is generally the case after an active campaign. Trotter much worse and in an alarming state.

December 27

Nothing particular has occurred in the interval between the 19th and this day. I have just received orders to march the Brigade to Alcains. Maxwell and I reconnoitred the road to a ford across the Ponsul yesterday and found it practicable if we have no rain before tomorrow or next day.

We have discovered some houses in Ladoeiro, 2 leagues hence

containing hay sufficient for 4 or 5 days more. We shall therefore take advantage of the fine weather to cross the ford and bring the horses back to eat the forage.

December 29

This morning I marched the Brigade by the road on the left bank of the Ponsul, but before we reached the ford 6 guns and 4 ammunition wagons stuck in the mud. Although the ground appeared firm and horses were not over their hoofs in the mud, yet the weight of the guns being so great, the road in a few minutes was like a quagmire. Every path was tried to the right and left for some distance and almost every carriage was dragged through by the men, which detained us 3 hours and was a work of great labour. It seemed to us as if the water from the higher ground had completely undermined the road in finding its way to the river - so after the first gun had sunk a little, water rose and made the ground in every direction nearly impassable. Some of the men sank above their knees and in galloping to the front to halt a gun which had been dragged through and was proceeding on the march, my horse's forelegs suddenly disappeared and I went over his head with mine, hat and feather almost buried in the mud. Such a condition we were all in! To a spectator unconcerned it would have been a great amusement to have seen our situation, but to me, the only officer and wishing to get to Escalos de Baixo before dark, it was no joke to be detained such a time.

Although we marched from Idanha-a-Nova at 9, we did not reach the ford till 3 o'clock in the afternoon. After crossing it we fed and began to ascend the hill by the pass leading to the village. We had only marched 2 leagues and had one more, but the horses were so exhausted with the fatigue they had already had and being deficient of 30, it was difficult to get any of the guns up this very steep hill. However we succeeded with all the carriages but two, which remained with a guard at the foot of the hill.

I determined on leaving the park with the gunners and going to the village with the horses, fearing the horses might suffer from being out in such cold weather after having been three weeks in crowded stables. Our guide undertook to show us the way and though we were only three miles from Escalos de Baixo, he led us about in the dark constantly marching from 6 till 10, when to our great surprise and vexation he brought us back to the guns again. When I saw the light of the guards' fire and, from its reflection the park, I really thought we had fallen in with some other Brigade. The stupid fellow of a guide had led us about and made a complete circle and brought us, after 4 hours, to the spot from which we started. We were obliged to picket our horses and with two blankets belonging to the sentries and an empty stomach, I took refuge in the bushes.

December 30

After a cold night's rest in my humble bed I rose with an appetite keener if possible than the morning air. One of the non-commissioned officers had some biscuit and with a little of it I made breakfast. The Drivers who last night had such a roundabout jaunt, having made a large fire, were anxious to punish the guide by giving him a roasting, which alarmed the poor fellow so much that he ran off in the greatest haste and did not look behind him till he reached the valley.

The two carriages had now been brought up the hill and we proceeded to Escalos de Baixo, a small village 3 leagues from Idanha-a-Nova, to which after getting some straw for the horses and quarters for the men, I returned with the former and the Drivers and was much concerned to find Lieutenant Trotter had died in the morning about 5 o'clock and as the Doctor had thought it necessary to bury him a few hours after, I was too late to have the satisfaction of attending his funeral. When I saw him yesterday morning he was better and I little expected such a change in so short a space of time (only 26 hours).

Three Corporals with a remount of the 28th horses [?] joined us this day.

January 2, 1813

The hay being consumed I marched the horses to Escalos de Baixo and from thence the whole Brigade to Alcains, one league further. This is a very pleasant village, larger and more comfortable than those

131

we have been in. There are several respectable families, but they are shy towards us so that we shall have no chance of getting acquainted. My Patrone and his family are civil enough and the Spanish Commissary to whom I have already alluded continues his attentions.

January 5

I went to Castello Branco, 2 leagues from Alcains (one of the principal towns of Beira). It is a Bishop's see and has been a place of great note. The houses are not good, except those of the Priests and some families who live outside the gates. The Bishop's Palace is a large irregular building displaying neither taste in architecture, nor in the apartments. The gardens are pleasant and are a great resource for those people who have permission to enter them. The number of statues of saints which are placed in rows at right angles to every part of the flower garden is so great that they almost hide the spot they are intended to ornament. On a hill looking over the town are the ruins of an old castle commanding the town and the several roads leading to it.

January 17

It being expected that General Alten's Brigade of Cavalry will be sent to Alcains, we received orders to leave it open for them and in consequence marched this day to Vila Povoa, 1 league distant and nearer the Serra da Atalaya. It is a small but not uncomfortable village and the houses are in good order, the French never having visited them. I had a snug quarter in the Priest's house and from the beauty of his nieces was half inclined to study Portuguese.

During my stay here I went to all the neighbouring villages: So Vicente da Beira where there is a monastery, Alpedrinha a large town and famous for wine, Tinalhas a small village near Vila Povoa and every other place within 3 leagues - a fine, bold country, very healthy and fertile.

A Court Martial

February 2

Maxwell having been summoned to appear before a General Court Martial at Coria, I was ordered to attend as one of the evidences in his defence and left Vila Povoa this day and slept at Idanha-a-Nova, 5.5 leagues away.

February 3

I went to Zarza la Mayor in Spain by Zibreira, 7 leagues and excellent quarters and was not a little pleased at being once more among Spaniards.

February 4

By Moraleja to Coria, 7 leagues; a pleasant ride and the weather was remarkably fine. I found Maxwell quite prepared for his trial and everyone confident of his acquittal.

February 5

At 9 am the Court assembled - some of the prosecution evidences were examined but they, being Portuguese, their examination was very tedious for want of a good interpreter.

February 6

The Court continued the proceedings and adjourned to Monday.

February 8

I attended the Cathedral on Sunday and was much pleased with the music. The tone of the organ is remarkably fine. The Band of one of the British Regiments assisted and the effect was very grand. On the terrace in front of the Cathedral, looking towards the river Alagon, are three tombstones to perpetuate the memory firstly of Colonel Wilson[4] of the 39th Regiment who also commanded a Brigade of Infantry in the last campaign and who died at Moraleja soon after the retreat to the frontier from the fatigue he had suffered during the severe weather we had been exposed to - and secondly of Colonel Stewart [5] of the 50th Regiment who also commanded a Brigade of Infantry during the latter part of the campaign and fell a victim to the effects of its hardships soon after his arrival at Coria. The third stone was to the memory of Staff Surgeon Mackintosh, [6] who died at Coria after 3 days illness contracted by his unintermitting attention to his profession, so soon terminated - perhaps from the hard life he had led.

Although permission was obtained to bury these officers under the terrace, yet the bigoted ideas of the clergy were not reconciled to it and seemed to think their holy ground would be contaminated by the interment of these heretics, and were much displeased that the tombstones were above the surface, their promenade being thereby interrupted, though they were not a foot above the level and quite at the end. I have no doubt that when the army quits their cantonments to take the field once more in defence of Spain, these bodies (of men who fell victim in her cause) will be removed and perhaps even not buried again.

The only thing striking within the Cathedral is the organ. Outside is an arched entrance, very ingeniously carved with images of all the Apostles, Saints, etc. and groups of figures describing the several interviews of our Saviour with the people; all in stone within the arch.

The building is close to the edge of the cliffs, under which the river Alagon formerly ran, but as over many seasons it was evident that the rapidity of the current continued to wash away the bank and undermine the rocks on which the Cathedral stands, it was resolved to turn the course of the river and it now runs about 500 yards further off. The bridge which formerly crossed the river remains and the ground under it is cultivated with little appearance of its ever having been the course of a river. Many people say the river was turned by a shock of earthquake and that the crack which is seen in the bridge is a proof of it. However this is very unlikely as the arches have not sunk in the least. [7]

The gardens near the Cathedral are very pleasant and contain some good fruit. The town is surrounded by an old Roman wall and was formerly defended by a strong tower with battlements which, from the excellence of the masonry and the nature of the stone are almost in a perfect state. The houses are in general good and the streets well paved, but the place is so infested with flies that it is quite proverbial and anyone going from Coria to another place is called Lexor Mascho, the Spanish for a fly.[8]

This day the prosecution closed and court adjourned to the 11th, when Maxwell appeared on his defence and several evidences in favour of it were called in, myself amongst the number. At 3pm the Court dissolved.

February 12
I dined with Sir Rowland Hill.

February 13
With Major Carncross,[9] and in the evening went to the Military Theatre. The play was 'The Poor Gentleman'. The house was very well fitted up, the scenery good. The performers played well and everything gave much satisfaction to a crowded audience. The officers concerned had a great deal to do in the preparations, as the building was an old convent going to ruins. The shops in town offered nothing which answered for the dresses, and such things as could not be collected amongst the officers of the Division and their wives (the few who were with them) were sent for from Lisbon.

February 14, Sunday
I crossed the Alagon in a ferry and went to Ceclavin, a large town 3 leagues from Alcantara, and from Coria 5 leagues. I dined with the Buffs who were quartered there and met my friend Farquharson. Nothing remarkable in the place.

February 15
I went to Alcantara, crossing the Tagus by a rope being fixed at each end on the opposite banks, a man pulling us across hand over hand. The stream is so rapid and irregular that this is the only way a boat can reach the opposite side. I afterwards crossed a stream which runs into the Tagus by an old bridge.

The town is old but the houses are more regularly built than any I have seen except in the larger places and the streets are well paved and generally broad. It is surrounded by a wall defended by redoubts and there are several detached works commanding the approaches.

The church or Cathedral is one of the most noted remains of antiquity, but the celebrated bridge crossing the Tagus and thrown from the banks of two very high hills surpasses everything of the kind I could have imagined. There are 6 arches and the height of the centre from the water is I believe 160 feet. One of the arches was destroyed about 5 years ago [10] in some of the operations between the French and the Portuguese, while the latter were retiring. It would be a work of immense labour to repair it, but as the passage of the Tagus at this point was considered necessary by Lord Wellington, he ordered the senior officer of the Staff, Major Sturgeon, [11] to contrive some means of rendering it passable. In three weeks, if I am not mistaken, he completed the work ordered, having ingeniously invented a rope-work of sufficient strength on such a principle as to support the weight of 24 tons.

He placed this flying rope bridge immediately over the broken arch and it answers every purpose and only requires the attendance of a man to prevent people or animals from meeting in the middle, as the action would become irregular and perhaps disengage some of the tackle.

Some of our city bucks or well fed alderman would be afraid to trust their carcasses to such an airy footing - it is not to be compared with Battersea Bridge for beauty and the grandeur perhaps might not attract their attention. I crossed it on the light fantastic toe and descended the banks of the hill as far as possible to look under the rope work and have an idea of the principle of its construction. [12]

The Tagus is narrow near Alcantara and the windings through its bed of rocks are very remarkable and beautiful. The side of the rock near the water's edge is of a purple colour and the reflection from it in the water while the sun shines gives the same appearance as we see in paintings of lakes in Italy, except where the current is rapid. I had a fine day for my observations and only regretted my inability to give a better idea by making a sketch of the scene than I can possibly contrive with my pen. I returned to my quarters, which were very good, and the next morning...

February 16

...I went to Rosmaninhal, 6 leagues, entering Portugal by a bridge across the Erjas near the castle of Segura. I bid adieu for a short time (I hope) to the comparatively clean houses and hospitable people of Spain and now prepared myself for filth and an uncomfortable hovel in a Portuguese village, which when I entered the quarter given me by the Juiz do Foro of Rosmaninhal, more than answered my sanguine expectations. However the people were civil and I was content.

February 17

I went to Monforte, a small village 3 leagues from Rosmaninhal, occupied by Whinyates' Troop of Horse Artillery. In my ride this day I remarked the very great improvement in agriculture occasioned by the evident necessity of a large supply of corn for the use of the people and the still greater encouragement of knowing the excellent market afforded by our Commissaries. The waste lands are clearing and the gumcistus which overruns such tracts of country are cut down to give place to corn. Several thousand acres I observed already in a forward state.

I dined with Whinyates and his officers and the next morning returned to the Brigade at Vila Povoa, 5 leagues, having made a pleasant tour of 178 miles. I found Litchfield [13] had joined the Brigade during my absence.

February 20

We went to Abrantes for some new wheels, harness, stores etc, in consequence of orders received from Headquarters.

Part Four
The Advance To The Ebro

WELLINGTON'S PLAN for the 1813 campaign required Sir Rowland Hill's Corps to join the main body at Moraleja on the river Huebra. Thereafter Wellington intended to cross the river Tormes, to turn the enemy's right flank and eventually to make contact with the Spanish Fourth Army (often referred to as the Army of Galicia) on the river Esla. The Anglo-Portuguese army numbered 77,000 of all ranks. The plan was ambitious and depended for its success on very careful timing.

Captain Webber's Journal records the moves of the 2nd Division in the opening stages of the brilliant series of operations which resulted in the crossing of the Ebro, the battle of Vitoria and the subsequent expulsion of the French from Spain.

The March Resumed: Coria And Plasencia

February 24

RECEIVED ORDERS to march to Ladoeiro, 6 leagues. The new wheels and harness not having arrived, I could only send one division,[1] which Litchfield took charge of. Received a letter from Maxwell with an account of the enemy having attacked one of our advanced posts near Bejar. It was defended by the 50th Regiment and some Portuguese; in all about 700 men, and the French brought up 1,100 with 100 Cavalry to take it (as they expected) by superior numbers. However they were repulsed with loss and without having gained any advantage.

March 2

Received the General Orders announcing Maxwell's full acquittal of both charges preferred against him.

March 5

Maxwell rejoined the Brigade and resumed command. He was received with three cheers from all the men.

March 6

Our new wheels and two new carriages with harness, stores etc arrived from Abrantes.

March 8

Marched to Escalos de Baixo, 2 leagues.

March 9

To Ladoeiro, 4 leagues, where we found Litchfield. A miserable village this, and the people not much improved since we marched there in December after our retreat. I had a dirty uncomfortable quarter and so cold that my deafness increased very much. As I found no chance of getting better while in it, I obtained leave to go to Castello Branco for a few days, where I had a snug room and a glass window and after four days care I found myself much relieved and returned to Ladoeiro.

March 21

Marched to Zibreira, 3 leagues, on the main road to Coria. This village is almost as bad as the last and every day I passed in it seemed tedious. Moore[2] joined the Brigade with 7 Gunners for the Company.

April 9

I went to Penamacor, a large frontier town situated on a hill defended formerly by fortified works which are now in ruins. I had appointed to meet my friend Smyth there and went by Idanha-a-Nova, the distance 9 leagues. I dined with Cairns and the officers of his Brigade, who had been quartered there some time, I saw nothing of Smyth.

April 10

Cairns and Bridges[3] returned with me to Zibreira where I found a letter from Smyth accounting for his not having come to meet me.

April 11

Cairns and Bridges left us.

April 18

Having represented the scarcity of forage, we received orders to march to Moraleja and marched this day across the Erjas to Zarza la Mayor in Spain, 3.5 leagues, thus taking leave of Portugal with very little wish of seeing it again. Captain Beane's[4] Troop of Horse Artillery had been the greater part of the winter in Zarza la Mayor and occupied it still.

April 19

Marched to Moraleja, 5 leagues. I had the best quarter in the place; the house of Don Immanuel Novasso, who had received as guests the Commander-in -Chief of both armies French and English) - a room about 50 feet long with the most comfortable bed I ever saw.

April 21

Went to Coria to see the play the of 'The Honeymoon'. Maxwell spoke the prologue and gave much satisfaction.

April 22

Returned to the Brigade.

April 23

Went to Puebla de Azaba to see my friend Smyth. Crossed the Sierra de Perales, 19 leagues and a very bad road.

April 24

Went to Fuenteguinaldo, 1 league, to see the officers of the 52nd Regiment. In returning saw and counted 30 large eagles feeding on a dead horse within pistol shot of me.

I took several rides round the neighbourhood of Puebla de Azaba with Jenkinson and the officers of the Troop and passed a very pleasant time, though not so long as I otherwise should have, as Smyth was unwell and unable to go out.

April 27

I returned to quarters, 7 leagues, through Morcillo and some other villages to see how the country was supplied with forage. Crossed two branches of the Alagon by bridges constructed by our Engineers. Had an excellent quarter in Galisteo and the next morning went to look about the town, which is surrounded by a wall about 40 feet high - very strong, but only for defence from Infantry.

The Alagon passes close under the wall and is crossed by a handsome bridge. Nothing but wheat grown near the place. The houses in the centre of the town are pretty good, but near the walls they are almost all in ruins, the French troops having pulled them down for firewood.

Went to Coria by the left bank of the river through Riolobos and two other villages and crossed in the ferry boat. This day rode 6 leagues. In the evening I attended the Theatre. The plays were "The Road to Ruin" and "The Bee Hive". Maxwell played in the former as Mr Silky and in the farce as Captain Ralton, in both of which he excelled.

April 30

I returned to Moraleja.

May 1

Marched to Coria, 2 leagues distant, to make room for the Conde do Amarante's Division of the Portugese Infantry. Dined with Sir Rowland Hill. On the 2nd, dined with Major Goldfinch and on the 3rd with Major Carncross.

May 4

Sir Rowland Hill inspected the Brigade on the Place near the town, after which we marched to Morcillo, 2 leagues, on the Plasencia road and on the right bank of the Alagon.

May 15

I sent a bill to Lisbon on the Commissary General for money payable to Mr Wood. We received a route to Oliva de Plasencia, two days march.

I went to Plasencia, through Galisteo, 6 leagues, and dined with Colonel Bunbury. The approach to the town, which is on an eminence in a beautiful valley, is very picturesque: the road, winding over hills and ravines where not a tree is to be seen, suddenly enters this fertile valley and when only a quarter of a league from the town the view changes as if by magic. The Cathedral, Bishop's Palace and Gardens, with several large buildings, are the most striking objects and the country is interspersed with pleasantly situated Quintas and several Chapels on the sides of the surrounding hills. The Alagon almost insulates the town and then finds its way through the mountains.

May 16, Sunday

The anniversary of the battle of Albuera [5] was celebrated by the troops here with great festivity. The streets appeared like groves, as from every window the soldiers had suspended large boughs of trees which almost reached the ground. The army has been so well paid lately that every man has plenty of money, and wine and music were the order of the day. The officers had grand dinner parties and the inhabitants seemed to participate in the general sentiment.

It was Sunday and the churches were crowded with people to hear Mass and to offer their prayers and thanksgivings for a miracle which had been performed, as they supposed, by the interference of their Saint. A piece of Church plate had been stolen from the altar of the Cathedral and nothing was heard of it till a few days ago, nor was suspicion attached to anyone. Some labourers in ploughing a field turned it up without injury and thinking it sacrilege to keep it, immediately carried it to the principal person of the Church. The recovery of this holy treasure was soon made known by proclamation, and public rejoicings, thanksgivings and illuminations - besides processions innumerable - were the consequence.

Every Sunday has been particularly solemnized and this was the last on which they intended to waste so much unnecessary expense and time. The Host was carried about in great style amidst ringing of bells and firing of squibs and rockets. Whosoever met it was by custom obliged to kneel till it had passed.

Englishmen are only required to take off their hats and lucky enough for us just then, as it entered the square while a large party of officers were lounging about, and continued in the same spot for 5 minutes and then moved a little but did not leave the square for an hour. From every window was displayed flags, large pieces of silk, variegated counterpanes, etc. There were images of our Saviour, the Virgin Mary and of the Saints posted at several doors and a grand Altar or Communion table covered with crimson velvet edged with gold lace was placed at the door to which the Host was carried.

Everyone knelt for some minutes to say a prayer and during the whole of the scene, the bells of all the Churches and Chapels were ringing in the most violent and confused manner and if a person had been coming to the town and had never witnessed anything of the kind, he would have set off at a gallop, supposing the people mad, or that the enemy was near, or that some dreadful fire had been discovered and these were the alarm bells to warn the people of their danger.

This grand festival afforded much amusement to the soldiers and they in their turn had large parties at their several quarters to entertain such of the inhabitants as they knew. I went to a party in the evening at the house of a family of large fortune where I saw some pretty women and was much gratified by hearing some delightful singing and music. The Band of the Buffs was there and we finished the evening by dancing.

SALAMANCA RECAPTURED

May 17

I took a walk on the Esplanade, which is outside the works of the town and is much frequented by the greatest people. At the end of it is a large aqueduct of several arches conveying water from the surrounding hills to the several fountains. I went to the Cathedral, which is very grand and to the Bishop's Palace, but could not get admission, it being too early. However I was informed there was nothing remarkable there.

The troops received orders to march towards Puerto de Baños and I joined the Brigade at Carcaboso, 2 leagues from Plasencia. They had marched to this village the day before - on the right bank of the Alagon, 3 leagues from Morcillo.

May 19

Marched to Jarilla, 4.5 leagues through Oliva and near Villar [de Plasencia], Sir Rowland Hill's quarters. The road to Jarilla for the last mile is impassable for Artillery and we left the guns at the bottom of the hill on which it stands and took the men and horses to the village.

May 20

To Gargantilla, 3 leagues, situated as was the last village on the side of the Sierra that runs up to Bejar. Left the guns parked at Aldeanueva on the high road. Headquarters at Baños.

May 21

3 leagues (through Baños) in the pass and bivouacked in a wood near the road, which was very bad and rough all the way from Aldeanueva [del Camino]. The town of Baños [de Montemayor] is in the most ruined state and the few houses remaining were occupied by the Staff of Headquarters.

May 22

To Valdefuentes [de San Ciusin], 2.5 leagues, clearing the Puerto de Baños without any damage to the carriages and encamped on ground near the village. Headquarters at Valdefuentes occupied. The advance-guard of our Cavalry was 3 leagues off. We heard that Lord Wellington had moved his Headquarters from Frenada on the day before.

May 23

Sir Rowland Hill reviewed the Corps.

May 24

Marched to Villaroba [?] and encamped in a wood, the whole of the Corps on the same ground, 3 leagues from Valdefuentes.

May 25

To Rozardos and encamped near it. Sir Rowland Hill and Staff in camp also. This day we marched 4 leagues. Lord Wellington's Headquarters at Tamames.

May 26

Information received that 4,000 of the enemy under General Villatte still occupied Salamanca. Our Cavalry and Horse Artillery had bivouacked in the same wood with us during the night and were sent on in different columns at 5 this morning to ascertain the enemy's force at Salamanca and at Alba de Tormes.

We marched at the same time on the main road and when 2 miles from the former town were halted, the enemy not having quitted the neighbourhood.

It seems General Villatte's information was so bad or that he took so little trouble to obtain any, that he hardly believed the report of the British army having quitted their cantonments on the frontiers; much less did he expect to see us overlooking the hill in front of his windows and not three miles off.

He was in the town; his troops were in camp near the village of Santa Marta on the left bank of the Tormes, 2 miles from him. Our Cavalry moved very quickly to attack them and they had only time to strike their tents and be off. The men had been carousing all the morning and were half drunk.

The General contrived to escape from the town and take the command of his Division. The river had risen so considerably in the night, owing to the heavy rain of the preceding day and the current was so rapid that he relied on the impossibility of our Cavalry following him. However he took up a position on the opposite hills to cover the retreat of his baggage, ammunition wagons etc, and fired several rounds from his two guns at our Cavalry and Horse Artillery in fording the river, but without any effect.

A fine piece of ground allowed them to follow at a gallop and Villatte retired at the same pace, sending his guns and Cavalry in front of his routed Infantry, instead of having them in the rear as a guard.

He abandoned 5 or 6 ammunition wagons, and some baggage also fell into our hands.

The troops of Horse Artillery under Captain Beane particularly distinguished themselves this day - everything was done by them alone. Not a man of the enemy was killed or wounded by our Cavalry and those taken were chiefly the drunken or infirm men who could not keep up the extraordinary speed with which the Infantry fled. Beane's guns fired a few rounds, then limbered up and off at a gallop to the next commanding spot, fired again and so on for about 2 leagues, frequently very far in advance of the Cavalry, who did not seem to enter into the spirit of the affair, although there seldom can occur a better opportunity for their action.

The enemy lost about 100 killed and 250 wounded and prisoners and had everything been properly managed or answered the expectations of Lord Wellington, who was present, scarcely a man of the column, 300 of which were Cavalry, ought to have escaped. (The prisoners say so and were surprised our cavalry did not charge.) The enemy went off in the direction of Avila to join part of their army of the centre, which had been there for some time and as our Cavalry and Horse Artillery had marched 8 leagues that day without a minute's halt, and no Infantry being up, Lord Wellington gave up the pursuit, which would anyway have interfered with his plans.

Lord W. was much annoyed at General Victor Alten's Brigade of cavalry not joining as he had ordered. They arrived too late to be of any use. He had while at Tamames received accurate intelligence of the enemy's force and their imagined security and he timed everything so well that the head of the column which marched from Ciudad Rodrigo arrived on the heights near Salamanca on one side, while we appeared on the other.

After the enemy had been driven from Santa Marta we crossed the Tormes, breast high and encamped on the right bank, near the ground an hour before occupied by the French.

The Division of General Silveira and the Conde do Amarante occupied Salamanca as did a large part of Castaños's [6] army. Lord Wellington, accompanied by Marshal Beresford and Staff entered it in the evening and established their Headquarters there.

I went to a dance at Colonel May's[7] house and being pretty well tired by a 6 league march under a smoking sun and the amusements of the evening, returned to the camp.

May 27

At 5 we marched on the road to Toro and halted 3 miles from Salamanca at the foot of an eminence on which were Lord Wellington and his Staff. As he had not seen Sir Rowland Hill's Corps for a considerable time, he took the opportunity of seeing us on the march and was much pleased with the appearance of the troops. After which we proceeded to ground near La Orbada, 5 leagues and encamped.

Lord Wellington returned to Salamanca.

CONSIDERATIONS OF STRATEGY

May 28

Halted. The plan of campaign thus far appears to have been to deceive the enemy with an idea of a part of the army marching on Madrid and in consequence, as it has answered, the enemy have kept a large force in that quarter. For a month or six weeks before we took the field, Lord Wellington had officers reconnoitreing towards Madrid by the Puerto del Pico, Talavera de la Reyna and Toledo and it is said he wrote to the Supreme Junta [8] requesting their assistance to the Commissariat Department of Sir Rowland Hill's Corps, which he intended should march that way - and relying on their patriotism and attachment to the general cause, to forward his intelligence as much as possible by obtaining the most correct information of the enemy's movements and keeping up a regular communication with the British Generals commanding.

This of course became known as he wished and the enemy acted accordingly. For a long time he thought this Corps would have marched to the Capital, while the rest of the army marched to Burgos.

After our arrival at Salamanca Lord Wellington continued to deceive the enemy by showing such a large force there, having his Headquarters with it and moving a part of Castaños's army on the road to Madrid through Alba de Tormes, which place (I forgot to mention) we took with a few prisoners on the 27th.

In the meantime Sir Thomas Graham [9] was moving to Zamora and Toro by Bragança and Lamego with the greatest part of the British army and the Hussars Brigade of Cavalry in order to form a junction, or open communications with the Galician army under Giron. He left his cantonments on the frontiers of Portugal about the 26th, having the 1st, 2nd, 3rd, 4th, 5th, 6th & 7th Divisions under his command. The Portuguese Division of Infantry under the Conde do Amarante marched on Salamanca and, by Lord Wellington being with them, the enemy naturally supposed the principal part of the allied army was there, instead of which the heart of it was with Thomas Graham, and their ignorance of its strength or movements, added to the excellence of Lord W.'s plan and the celerity of its execution, seemed already to foretell the enemy's defeat and gave spirit to everyone but them.

The enemy had constructed redoubts and taken every measure to strengthen the extensive position from Zamora to Toro on the right bank of the Douro and from all accounts it is very formidable. However Sir Thomas Graham's instructions are, we hear, to turn the right of it if possible and everything seems to go on so well that we expect he will, before the enemy can collect a force sufficient to make any stand against him.

Till something is done by him we cannot move, as the position is too strong to attack in front, protected as it is by the Douro running close to the foot of the hills. Lord Wellington is in high spirits, much pleased with the effective state of the army and is very sanguine in his expectations.

May 29

Lord Wellington left Salamanca to visit Sir Thomas Graham, who he supposed would be that day at Miranda do Douro. The distance is

14 leagues and while the enemy thinks he is with us, they will have the agreeable surprise of seeing him at the head of near 30,000 British troops immediately in front of them.

May 31

I went to Salamanca and dined at a coffee house with Cairns and his officers. Afterwards I went to see a review of Castaños's army, about 16,000 strong on the plains near the Toro road. There were a great many spectators and the troops made a very fine appearance: well dressed and well fed.[10] In the evening Castaños gave a grand ball and supper to which I was invited, but not having my ball dress I could not go, which I regretted very much as it was the most splendid entertainment given in the town for many months and was attended by all the beauty and rank of Salamanca.

June 1

In the morning I visited the Cathedral, but it did not strike me as being so handsome as I had been led to suppose, though it surpasses all others I have seen in the country except those of Toledo and Astorga. The architecture is grand but the interior is not remarkably so. The Irish College is a very fine building now converted into barracks for the soldiers. The convents, monasteries and most of the places of worship are in ruins and many buildings inside the walls were destroyed by the French last year, or by the fire of our artillery directed to them while occupied by their troops.

The Square is one of the handsomest of any town in Spain. The houses are of fine stone and built with the greatest uniformity. All the ground floors are occupied by shopkeepers and the second stories, projecting 10 or 12 feet, form a Piazza which is a gay promenade and an agreeable shelter from the heat of the sun. Outside the Square is a large market place where vegetables, fruit, butter etc. were in abundance, but dear owing to the number of troops in the town. The houses are pretty good and those of the principal families are excellent.

When Lord Wellington entered the place in the last campaign he was received with such unbounded marks of joy, but the unfortunate inhabitants have during our absence in the winter suffered very seriously. The French levied contributions without mercy. The troops were allowed to plunder and commit every kind of outrage for two days after their arrival and the distress of the people is said to have been inconceivable. Had the enemy been earlier apprised of our approach the other day I have no doubt the same excesses would have marked their departure. Happily for the people, they had scarcely time to take themselves away. However, the dread of their returning and experiencing again such misery made them shy in welcoming our last entrance, though individually they seem much attached to the English and to their own country.

The town was so crowded with troops that I thought there was no chance of getting a billet and slept in a part of a ruined convent which Cairns had taken possession of for his Brigade - his house standing in the cloisters. Besides Castaños's army there were the Brigade of Household Cavalry, some Portuguese Infantry, Colonel Tulloh's two Brigades of Portuguese Artillery and Cairns's of British.[11]

After having seen everything I could, though in too great a hurry to give a good account of any, I returned to the camp of La Orbada where I heard that General Graham had crossed the Douro and turned the enemy's right - that they (the French) had not destroyed the bridge at Toro, and seemed to have been quite unprepared for the arrival of this force. Large patrols of their Cavalry continued to remain in our front about 2 leagues from La Orbada and caused two or three alarms, when the troops were immediately assembled. Lord Wellington was expected to be at Toro this day.

CROSSING THE DOURO

June 2

The Light Division, which had been encamped about a league from us marched this day for Toro and the Portuguese joined us. In the afternoon also arrived the Brigade of Lifeguards and Cairns' Brigade of Artillery from Salamanca. Orders were given for our march.

June 3

We left the Camp for Villabuena [del Puente], passing through Fuentesauco where we were cheered with loud 'Viva's' and ringing of bells. We encamped on a plain near Villabuena, without a tree either for shelter or firewood. We had marched 6 leagues, the weather intensely hot and we could get no shade. The men had to go 2 miles to an old vine plantation and collect the stubble or pieces of sticks, which had been placed there to be burnt (for the benefit of the smoke and ashes to the ground), and it was a long time before they could cook their dinners.

This day we were informed of a gallant affair which took place the day before between the Hussars and some French Cavalry, the result of which was the capture of 200 men and horses and the death of several of the enemy. On our part we lost Lieut Cotton, a fine young man of the 10th Dragoons, and a few men. The prisoners, under Portuguese escort, passed us soon after our arrival on this ground and I never saw stouter or finer looking fellows.

In a conversation with one of their officers, I was told that the condition of our Cavalry and Artillery horses quite astonishes them and that with the shoals of men (as he terms our army) which Lord Wellington has with him, it would be quite impossible for the French to make any stand against us. Certainly no Cavalry could have taken the field in finer order, but as for the force Lord Wellington has, he will find sufficient employment for them in getting the enemy out of the many strongholds they have in the country.

The account of the affair between the Hussars and French Cavalry reached us in the evening. Their advanced pickets were near Zamora and their officer and 30 men were taken, after which the Hussars went to Toro from whence the enemy Cavalry retired to Morales [de Toro], one league from any good road, closely pursued. When near the village the Hussars halted to give their horses breath and the enemy, supposing this to be in consequence of some orders to give up the pursuit, and flattering themselves that their own superiority in numbers was the cause, wheeled about and made for our Horse at a gallop. However to their astonishment, when within 20 paces the latter advanced at speed, charged through their line and, wheeling about, divided them and took the number of prisoners I have mentioned. The rest got off by their horses being fresh.

It is said Sir Thomas Graham crossed the Douro in two columns, one at Torrencen Corvo [12] by a pontoon bridge constructed by our Engineers, the other by a bridge at Miranda do Douro and afterwards crossed the Esla by a pontoon bridge. The former column has moved on Bragança and Benavente to open a communication with the Galician army, the latter has completely turned the enemy's strong position from the Esla to the Pisuerga and marched on Toro after taking a large quantity of provisions at Zamora - and are now going in the direction of Palencia.

Lord Wellington left Toro this morning or yesterday and expects to be in Valladolid tomorrow. Joseph Buonaparte's court has been held there during the winter and it is supposed he had not yet quitted it, but has a force of 10,000 men in the neighbourhood with which he is expected to make a stand. The Light Division is marching to some advanced ground and we hear has had a skirmish with the enemy's outposts.

June 4

God save the King [13]. We marched to the banks of the Douro, 3 leagues, and forded it a little above the bridge, which the enemy had destroyed previous to their retreat and though repaired in a temporary manner for the passage of our Infantry, no Horse could go over and all animals were obliged to ford. It was almost too deep for mules and ponies and two or three were carried down the stream. It was much more than chest high to our horses and we had a handful in getting the guns and ammunition wagons across - particularly the latter as, being a larger body and lighter, the current was more felt. Almost all our baggage was wet, but we were more fortunate than several who had lost theirs entirely.

The Brigade proceeded to Morales [de Toro] and I went into Toro to purchase wine etc. It was a beautiful day, though very warm and all the people had assembled to see the troops pass. Bells were ringing and every demonstration of joy given by them.

The town, standing on a hill, has a very fine view of the course of the Douro winding at its foot. The plain in front shows several roads leading to the bridge, the ascent from which is by a steep road, commanded at different points by small strong redoubts and there is a very strong tête du pont to guard the passage of the bridge.

The gates of the town had been loop-holed and the several approaches barricaded. Nothing was omitted which would render the place as defensible as possible and it is fortunate for us that we entered it so quietly. There is a large old Church, two convents and a town hall, but very few other large buildings. The shops were well supplied with all kinds of necessary articles and the market stocked with vegetables and fruits. The greatest luxury was the iced cream and lemonade sold by a Frenchwoman and made in perfection.

As Castaños had sent for quarters and is so beloved by the Spaniards, everyone crowded near the gates to see him arrive. Bells were ringing and at last he appeared, escorted by a party of his Cavalry. He was received by all ranks with the loudest acclamations - ladies cheering him from their windows and waving their handkerchiefs to him as he passed.

In the evening Morillo [14] was expected at the head of his 6,000 troops and being equally liked by the people and the army he was acclaimed in the same manner. As his Regiments arrived he formed them in succession in the Square, made them give the general salute to Castaños, who was in one of the houses, and then ordered them to be billeted off on the inhabitants. As there were several Regiments, this ceremony occupied a long time and gave me an opportunity of seeing all the Grandees who were posted in the windows of every storey of each house. I enjoyed myself more than Morillo could, for whichever way he turned to speak to his officers and men he was almost stunned with the 'Viva's' which resounded from the shrill tongues of women and children.

The ladies were elegantly dressed and their beauty was the most pleasing part of the scene. There was to be a ball and supper to welcome the arrival of Castaños and Morillo, but I could not stay though I had a promising invitation from a Spanish officer, and having purchased what I wanted, mounted my horse and set off for Morales.

Outside the walls of Toro was the Brigade of 18-Pdrs[15] which Lord Wellington intends to use in the field. They have come on so far very well. Morales is a pleasant village and I found our Brigade in a wood 2 miles from it. The day's march 4 leagues, fine open country and excellent roads.

THE FRENCH OUTFLANKED

June 5

Marched to Wamba, 4.5 leagues, passing through Torrelobaton and several other villages where we were welcomed by the ringing of bells and cries of 'Viva' from all the people. Encamped in a plain near the village. An officer of the Hussars with a patrol of 6 or 8 men were surprised here last night by an enemy picket and taken.

About this time we heard that the Alicante army under General Sir John Murray had embarked to make a diversion by landing on the coast of Catalonia and as it has a large battering train, it is supposed Lord Wellington intends to besiege either Tarragona or Barcelona.

Soult is said to be marching towards us with 20,000 men to form a junction with King Joseph previous to our bringing him to action (if possible), but Lord Wellington I believe is pretty confident on anticipating his moves.

Before we left Coria we received the account of an action between Suchet and General Murray, in which the latter gained some advantage and drove Suchet back to his former position; but everyone agreed in

157

the opinion that if the business had been well managed, Suchet ought to have paid very dearly for his temerity, as our position in front of Alicante is very strong. Great expectations were formed of this expedition, sent from Lisbon in June last and with the addition of the army from Sicily composed of 20,000 men who after landing were joined by 7 or 8,000 Spaniards. General M. was the last man in the army to whom such a command should have been entrusted and I hope for his and his country's sake he may never again be employed with equal responsibility.[16]

The French army of the centre has been withdrawn from Madrid and all detachments have been called in to make the Grand Army as strong as they can. They are supposed to be 6 leagues from us and our advance-guard is close to them. Our army was never in such order, such health, better equipped or better supplied than at present and the fatigues of this constant marching are lightly felt.

June 6

Marched to Mucientes, 5 leagues. The Cavalry, Horse Artillery and Cairns' Brigade of Artillery left us this morning, taking the great road to Peñaflor [de Hornija], while we moved on Valladolid by a cross-country road over a high common from which we had a good view of several large villages - Peñaflor on our left and Zaratan on our right, and two others whose names I could not learn.

Joseph Buonaparte quitted Valladolid only last night in the greatest confusion, taking all the plunder and treasure he had collected which, with his baggage, filled 60 cars. He did all the damage time would allow and destroyed the famous bridge across the Pisuerga. Lord Wellington entered this morning and immediately after left on the Burgos road as the enemy had retired so rapidly. His Headquarters were to be this evening at or near Palencia. The enemy left several of their sick in the hospitals and many lingerers or deserters were found in the town, besides 1 officer and 14 men of ours who had been there some time as prisoners.

We left Valladolid to our right and, as Mucientes is 2 leagues from it and as we had arrived a day late, I could not go there. I was much disappointed as I had heard it represented as one of the handsomest towns in Spain.

Maxwell left the Brigade in the morning and, having leave, he went there and on his return gave such a description of the place and its beauties that I regretted more than before my inability to gratify myself. The houses are of a very superior kind and the shops were filled with articles of every description, useful and ornamental - fish, fowls, meat, butter, eggs etc, in abundance in the market, capital hotels affording every comfort and luxury, French cooks, dinners dressed in their style, pastry cooks' shops, people of all trades. In short everything in the same state in which it had been previous to our approach, except the Palace, which Joseph had occupied and that was much damaged: the tapestry torn, pictures and glasses broken and everything valuable and portable carried away by King Jo's servants and soldiers.

The Court having been here all the winter, shops were filled with goods from France, so that it was in every respect a complete French town. All the French Party had taken lodgings there and it has been the scene of gaiety for some months - balls, routs and plays etc without end.

The Cathedral is very handsome and well worth seeing. The squares are formed by good houses and the streets are broad and well paved. On the banks of the river is a very pleasant walk in a shady avenue of chestnut trees, much resorted to every evening by the genteel people. The French Party has always been very strong here and when Lord Wellington entered last year, after the famous battle of Salamanca, he was received very coolly; so much had all classes been influenced by the example of a few French partisans who by their intrigues had almost made them forget the cause in which the country is engaged.

Lord Wellington's entrance to Madrid, which had been the residence of King Joseph and his Court, was marked with the most enthusiastic joy: illuminations for three nights, publick festivals, assemblies and balls the whole time he remained there. The French had a strong Party there also, but after our retreat Joseph went to Valladolid and has been there ever since, more convinced of the attachment of the people there than in the Capital.

June 7

Marched to Dueñas, 4 leagues, passing through Cigales, a large town, soon after which we entered the Royal road from Valladolid to Burgos. We encamped on the right bank of the Pisuerga, which ground the French only quitted the night before, closely pursued by our advancing Cavalry.

The town of Dueñas, situated on the side of a hill, has a large convent and a handsome Church, but the French have destroyed many of the houses and most of the others were deserted by the inhabitants. The country and neighbourhood is a complete vineyard and almost every house had a large cellar filled with excellent wine, but the doors were immediately broken open and what the French could not drink they threw away to prevent our tasting it, which was fortunate as our men could not have withstood the temptation it would have been and we should have had everyone intoxicated.

The course of the river has been turned a little above Dueñas and the bridge which crossed it from the town gates remains, the ground under it being perfectly dry; the river runs 500 or 600 yards further out, in the same way as at Coria. This is said to have been the effect of an earthquake, which is very possible, as the turning is so far from the bridge that it might not have been injured by the shock.

June 8

Marched to Torquemada, 5 leagues, crossing the Pisuerga by a bridge which the enemy had blown up but which has been repaired by our Engineers within the last 24 hours. I went to Palencia, a large and handsome town, 1.5 leagues to the left of the Burgos road. It has a handsome Church but there are no squares or any remarkable buildings. The gateways are handsome, one particularly elegant at the [main] entrance.

From Valladolid a Royal road branches off from the great Burgos road about two leagues from the town, passes through Palencia and then branches off on the opposite side in two directions, one leading towards La Coruña and the other back into the Burgos road.

I dined with a very pleasant family. The father is one of the principal magistrates; the daughter, and only child, very beautiful and accomplished. I gave her some hopes of returning to settle myself in Palencia. In the evening joined the Brigade.

June 9

Marched from the ground near Torquemada along the right bank of the Pisuerga to a shady wood, 2.5 leagues only. The 1st Brigade and Light Companies crossed at Torquemada to join the Cavalry in a reconnaissance. The town was in a most deplorable and ruinous state. The greater part of the houses having been pulled down to furnish materials for the several works constructed by the enemy for making a stand, which gave great proof of their ingenuity and perseverance.

The Church, situated close to the bridge, had been rendered a most formidable tête du pont. It was surrounded by a broad ditch and palisades and a loop-holed parapet and was itself a complete castle, which would have been difficult to take without breaching the walls. The road to Burgos passes by it and leads over the bridge to the left bank of the river. The route we took was in a different direction and the road was very bad and the rain made it in some parts very deep, almost impassable for heavy Artillery.

I forgot to mention that on the morning of the 7th the advance guard of one of our columns (the 4th and 7th Divisions) entered the town of Palencia at one gate while the rearguard of one of the enemy's columns marched out at the other, so close did Lord Wellington follow them. They lost no prisoners I believe, and very little baggage and as our troops had marched a great distance, they were not ordered to follow them, but encamped on the ground which the enemy had quitted half an hour before.

June 10

We continued our march up the right bank of the river through a very deep, bad road to a village [Astudillo?] and crossed the river [Pisuerga] by a fine stone bridge to Balbases, 3 leagues.

June 11

Marched to ground 1 mile from Castrojeriz, 1 league only, the enemy retiring to Burgos and assembling a large force in its neighbourhood. Lord Wellington arrived at Castrojeriz late in the afternoon after having reconnoitred the enemy's force and position. The town, though the Capital of a district is remarkable for nothing but filth and may be called a little Lisbon.[17]

We had the unexpected satisfaction of hearing this day that Sir Thomas Graham, of whose movements we had been ignorant, had secured the passage of the Ebro near San Martin [de Lines] and only awaited further instructions. Lord Wellington was in high spirits and his Staff said he was very sanguine in hopes of complete success attending his plans, which the army only knew when they were carried into execution.

The enemy's position on the Ebro was now turned and whether we besiege Burgos or not a great point has been gained which they were not prepared for.

THE FALL OF BURGOS

June 12

We marched towards Burgos, the enemy having taken up a position about 3 leagues from Castrojeriz and in front of Burgos. Colonel Ashworth's Brigade of Portuguese Infantry and Colonel O'Callaghan's[18] of British, with two guns of ours, were detached under the command of Colonel Ashworth on the road to Hormaza, also the German Hussars of General Fane's Brigade. General Stewart,[19] with the remainder of the Corps under Sir Rowland Hill, moved to the right to turn the left flank of the enemy's position by crossing the Arlanzon, while the Light Division and two Brigades of Cavalry made a flank movement in the night to turn their right - our column marching to attack them in front.

After passing through two or three villages, where the peasantry varied very much in their estimates from 5,000 to 20,000 as the strength of the enemy, we reached the village of Hormaza, close to a branch of the Arlanzon and on the heights opposite appeared the enemy in large force, with two light guns posted to command the road by which we were to advance.

Our Cavalry skirmishers were sent out and several were wounded on both sides. We remained quiet but on the alert, while Wellington waited for the Light Division and Cavalry to gain their destination and for another Brigade of Cavalry with a Troop of Horse Artillery to get in the rear of the enemy's line by marching some distance round. He passed us twice and seemed as cool and as much at ease as if taking a morning ride.

After two hours halt the order arrived for us to advance and as the enemy saw their left turned, they retired and we marched up the hill without opposition. On reaching the summit the view exceeded anything I can describe: about 6,000 British Cavalry formed in columns and our two Brigades of Infantry on one part of this elevated plain and, in front, about 6,000 of the enemy's Infantry covered by Cavalry and Artillery. In retiring they formed hollow squares and into one of them the German Hussars charged and took a gun and a few prisoners.

We followed them till they crossed the Arlanzon, on the opposite bank of which they took up another position and were joined by 5 or 6 thousand more. Except for another charge of Cavalry, the result of which was the capture of a second gun, the day finished with a brisk cannonade from Major Gardiner's [20] Troop of Horse Artillery, answered by the Artillery of the enemy, while they were in the meantime retiring on Burgos, but keeping a strong column to protect the bridge across the river, which would have cost us too many men to have retaken and interfered with Lord Wellington's arrangements.

On this high plain while the weather was fine and clear, all our force and that of the enemy seemed displayed as at a review. In the distance and very clear to the eye were seen the walls and castle of Burgos, with the grand spires of the Cathedral and several large Churches. The setting sun added very much to the grandeur of the scene, but all became suddenly darkened and the most tremendous thunder storm damped the pleasures of the day. It seems Lord Wellington showed this large force of Cavalry to give the enemy an idea that the greatest part of the army was marching on Burgos, as they would naturally conclude we had Infantry in proportion and during the affair he seemed anxious they should see the whole of the Cavalry, as they were formed in Brigade after the enemy retired across the river, and took up ground on the riverside brow of the hill.

I had not the good fortune of getting my two guns to bear on the enemy, but remained on the brow with the Cavalry. I was quite near enough and could have opened a fire with effect, but the fire of the Horse Artillery answered the purpose of annoying their rearguard.

Our loss was very trifling in this affair and had it not been for the disagreeable evening, ladies even would have ...

General Stewart's column did not arrive in time to effect the intention of turning the right of the enemy, nor did the Light Division arrive at the point intended for them so soon as was expected - otherwise in all probability we should have taken the greater part of this force prisoner. Many difficulties presented themselves in the advance, which was the cause of these two columns being delayed.

About 5 o'clock we began to move off to get the troops in bivouac in the valley. Lord Wellington went to a village two miles from Hormaza and our column went there also. I managed to get the men and horses under cover in an old castle and, all the apartments in the castle being in good repair, Cubitt [21] and myself got a comfortable room, but unluckily the French had carried off or destroyed all the beds. Our march this day, exclusive of manoeuvreing, was about 3.5 leagues (making General Stewart's about 5.5) and the ground being very heavy and the roads exceedingly bad in several places, our horses had a hard day's work. To our men and ourselves, interested in the movements, it was nothing.

June 13

At 5 o'clock this morning we heard a great explosion from the direction of the bridge and concluded the enemy had destroyed the works and evacuated the place, in consequence of their having received information of the turning of their right by General Graham's column, which by this time had crossed the Ebro near San Martin. In a short time we had the pleasure of hearing our opinions were well founded and that the enemy had withdrawn the garrison, retiring towards Pancorvo.

Whether this had any influence on our immediate movements I cannot say, as there were various conjectures as to Lord Wellington's intentions - some thinking he would have left a blockading force of Spaniards to watch the garrison of Burgos, while he with the whole of the British army pushed on to bring the enemy to action. This I thought most probable, as another siege of so strong a fortress would have diminished his British troops too much with the loss they would have sustained. I think he moved so near Burgos merely to make a feint, in hopes of deceiving the enemy, while he intended forming a junction with General Graham the other side of the Ebro and opening a communication with Bilbao and Santander, from whence he would easily receive the supplies for his army and the Battering train for the siege of any place he wished. The enemy certainly have supposed the greater part of our army to be with Lord Wellington and till now perhaps had no idea of any force being in their rear.

The objective was now gained and the whole army felt the greatest satisfaction at the intelligence of the destruction of the castle and citadel of Burgos, which we had looked forward to as ultimately to have been the grave of so many of our friends. Lord Wellington, we hear, is in high spirits on the occasion.

About 10 o'clock we left Hormaza and the different bivouacs occupied by the troops yesterday and marched in the same direction (Frias) as General Stewart's column. The remainder of Sir Rowland Hill's Corps had, as I have already mentioned, removed on to a road a great deal to the right of our line of march (by our having turned to the left). The roads were very heavy owing to the rain in the night. We could only march about 3 leagues today. We took up ground in the village of ..., the Cavalry and Horse Artillery bivouacking in a wood.

June 14

We continued our march in the same direction, through a very difficult pass, a distance of 6 leagues (to the neighbourhood of Montorio), which from the nature of the country and almost the worst roads I have seen, detained us from 4 in the morning till near 6 in the evening, when we halted and bivouacked 1 league from the village of Masa, Lord Wellington's Headquarters.

We marched in regular order, preceded by the Cavalry and one Regiment of Infantry, and the rest of the Corps followed in our rear and though the roads were so bad as to prevent more than three men going abreast - and sometimes even they were obliged to file through parts covered with large pieces of rock - yet we kept up with those in front. The General Officers and others gave us great credit for the attention we paid.

Three or four of our wheels suffered and the wheel horses were much shaken, but we met with no accident. We found that by coming this way we had turned the position of Pancorvo [22] on the Ebro, which the enemy had expected us to attack, from necessity (as they thought) through marching on that road. The peasantry told us they had never seen artillery travel through the pass as we did this day and we supposed the enemy were not aware of its being practicable, especially as the heavy rain had made it so much worse.

Our Cavalry were detached in every direction to reconnoitre the country and to protect our flanks, but I believe not a Frenchman is to be seen in the neighbourhood of our line of march. In the marches of the three last days we have crossed some hills and the face of the country is very different from that around Salamanca and Castrojeriz. There we had plain sailing and in general good roads. Here on the contrary they are so rough and narrow that without care and good driving and having the best materials, our carriages could not bear the constant shaking.

We heard that General Graham, having crossed the Ebro, is

marching down the left bank: we expect therefore to meet him in a day or two. The country near Vitoria is difficult and affords several excellent positions which the enemy know how to avail themselves of and we hope Lord Wellington may be able to bring them to action before they reach them.

THE COMMISSARIAT

June 14 (cont)

Our army was never more healthy, indeed I should think troops in England cannot be in a better state. Marching to a certain degree agrees with most men if the weather is favourable and they are well supplied. Rain is much more tolerable than dry weather if exposed to a vertical sun, as we were last year in the South. Since we left Toro I have not found the heat oppressive and my cloaks defend me from the wet. The soldiers have tents and although they are much crowded (one only being allowed for 20 men) the nights are sufficiently cool to prevent their feeling any ill effects from that cause. During the last campaign they had none and it was very trying to the strongest constitution to lie down, after a long march, exposed to the mists or dampness of the night air.[23]

It is a pleasure to be in an army so well regulated as this, in which the wants of the soldiers are so much considered and while every department, particularly the Commissariat, is established on such an excellent system.

In the retreat from Salamanca to Ciudad Rodrigo in November last, our Commissariat were very negligent with a few exceptions and many men, particularly Portuguese are supposed to have been almost starved to death. I know that many fell into the enemy's hands merely because of want of provisions: they became exhausted and at last were obliged to sit down by the roadside till death closed their eyes or the enemy were generous enough to procure conveyance to any of their hospitals.

I know also that some Portuguese soldiers received as rations ten chestnuts a man, which perhaps preserved their lives, as they have not the persevering spirit of the Spaniards, nor the heart of any Englishman to bear them up under difficulties and they were generally too indolent to mount an oak tree for acorns - by which many of our men made a hearty meal. Officers also thought them edible. I used to eat a great many by choice and there are some of the most delightful flavour.

Our Commissary was a most attentive man and I dare say our Brigade was the best provided in the army, and he assisted many others. But Lord Wellington, being so fully convinced of the great neglect in the department, dismissed several of its officers very soon after the army reached the frontiers of Portugal.

The great loss of the army in that retreat may be imputed to their bad management. An army must always suffer more or less when retiring before an enemy superior in every respect, but particularly in Cavalry as was the case, but while we were not above 12 leagues from Ciudad Rodrigo where there was a great Depôt, we certainly expected to see supplies of bread and biscuit much sooner that we did. The punishment I have mentioned proved a salutary lesson and I hope we may never hear of such another being necessary. Now the men live better than the Commissaries and they (the latter) ought not for a moment to forget the wants of others.

Our prospects are now so cheering and the campaign becomes so interesting that I would not relinquish the hope of seeing its termination on any account and I trust my health will enable me to bear the fatigue.

CROSSING THE EBRO

June 15

We marched through Masa, a small miserable village, where Lord Wellington's Headquarters had been for the last night, through ... to Poza de la Sal, near which we bivouacked in a wood and meadow. The road this day's march is much better than yesterday's, but very rough. The distance was 5 leagues.

June 16

We marched in high spirits at the thought of crossing the Ebro, towards Puente Arenas. The Light Division had been encamped not far from us in the night and they were to reach the banks of the river first so that we should not delay their march through the pass. The country for the first two leagues was open and the roads good till we reached the old chapel at the brow of a tremendous hill we had to descend. This chapel was nearly full of excellent salt and had been a Depôt of the French army.

A proportion of men from each Regiment were allowed to quit the ranks and get as much as they could carry for themselves and comrades. But although every man who entered the chapel filled his haversack, pockets and handkerchief, there was still sufficient for 5,000 men more. Salt is a scarce article except in the neighbourhood of the several salt works.

Owing to the danger of travelling[24] and the difficulty of transport, there are few adventurers to convey the necessary articles to such places where they may be most required and this is the reason of our paying so extraordinarily highly for everything. The Guerrillas carry off every animal they see unless protected by a greater number of men than they may have in their party. Those horses and mules that escape their vigilance and are fit for service are embargoed by the Spanish officers, or by people authorised by government to keep up their efficiency in Cavalry and Artillery. We seldom therefore met a traveller, except those employed in the Service, nor even in towns have we seen a carriage in motion.

Where war has not carried its miseries, the people still retain some remains of ancient grandeur and opulence, though the heavy contributions levied on every district have reduced their fortunes and their pride. We are now I hope laying the foundation of their future happiness and beginning to restore them to their rights. Let the crossing of the Ebro be hailed in their annals and be the omen of the downfall of the French despotism and oppression.

We now began the descent of the hill and to prepare for accidents and disasters to our carriages. Although the road was paved and rather broad, it would have been impossible to have moved without infantry to hold with the drag ropes. General Stewart gave us two Companies of the 71st and by great care we succeeded in reaching the valley without any accident. Had we locked our wheels, as is the plan in some Brigades, I think not a carriage would have escaped injury and perhaps several might have been totally disabled.

I never saw anything so tremendous as this pass, so steep that even with the assistance we had, the wheel horses frequently fell on their hocks and it was with the greatest difficulty we prevented the carriages from running over the side of the pavement - in which case they would have been precipitated (in some parts) 30 or 40 feet, and horses and drivers must have been killed.[25]

This descent is about three miles, but is not so steep after the first mile. We then entered a ruined village, which must once have been a beautiful retired spot. The change of scene was very great. After rocks and barren hills on each side, we entered the most fertile valley that can be imagined. Several small villages to the right and left; the largest has some excellent houses and seems an enviable place. The river was not in sight and we almost feared we had got to climb up the hills in front and descend by such another pass to reach it.

At last, after going a mile in a narrow lane with gardens and cornfields and vineyards on each side, we saw the bridge, the Puente Arenas. As we crossed, every man felt proud of the day and of the genius of Lord Wellington by whose skill and rapidity in execution we had been led thus far without any material opposition.

The river is narrow near the bridge and not very deep, but it varies very much in breadth and depth a little higher up. The village of ... is on the left bank, the bridge leading into it. We saw very few inhabitants and those did not cheer us or give any proof of our being welcome visitors. We had not met with any civility or marks of attachment to the cause since we left Palencia. French intrigue and a subdued spirit seem to have changed the people and they appear no longer enthusiastic or anxious to make the sacrifices necessary for regaining the liberty of their country.

Our march was by a winding road up the left bank and after surmounting a steep hill close by the waterside, nothing could exceed the romantic and beautiful scenery which presented itself and it would be useless to attempt any description. General Stewart, who commands the Division of Infantry, said he had travelled through most parts of Europe celebrated for their natural beauties, and on the banks of the Rhyne [sic] in particular, but he never saw anything to surpass the grandeur of this.

Now and then it was closed by inaccessible rocky mountains, whose tops seemed almost to touch and were as if separated by some convulsion of nature. The veins of marble, granite and other kinds of strata corresponded on each side of these deep and ... *{Here the Journal breaks off}*.

APPENDIX

The following documents were amongst Colonel Webber's papers

I: A Letter to Mr Webber

The prosperity of friends is certainly the cordial drop of existence, as we have experienced in observing the gratified expression of your noble Captain's phiz, who at the time must have prudence. I played the Commanding Officer and directed him to leave his card of thanks with General Phipps on the following morning. The General called the following morning to say how happy he was to have been instrumental in promoting Mary Anne's suit to Lord Mulgrave, but that Captain Webber actually owed his success to his own merits, which had obtained for him the high approbation of Lord Layndock [sic] & Hill; and General Dickson told Lord Mulgrave that there was not an officer of the same standing in the service on whom he would place greater dependence. His deserts are now properly known and estimated & I trust will be duly supported. Lord M.'s department is I believe the only one conducted impartially.

How will yours and the dear old Ken's hearts exult on this occasion! We dispatched our hero at 5 o'clock this morning, after giving him a maternal buss and blessing, and my sweet Poll's cheek glowed with satisfaction when she presented it to him, tho' her complection had never recovered from the effect of the blow which she received on her head in Gloucestershire. Her palidness your son modestly attributes to her love for himself, which he kindly promises to reward on his return from his continental affairs of gallantry, which from the fascinations of his person and manner have accumulated beyond what he was aware of!

173

I took care that our Uncle of Broad Street should be fully informed of the light he is held in by the Big Wiggs, which has so flattered him that he generously presented him with £20. There's an event for you worth recording!

And now for my dear George, who was announced with his Aunt Taylor. Rejoiced were we to see the blooming boy transmogrified into a bronzed tan of the hardy young man. He promised to dine with us next Sunday when I am to take him to Roseberry's, who still retains her partiality for him.

Captain Webber told me that he had enclosed you some of Brother's canvassing cards for a seat in the Direction and I am convinced that you will promote his interests if you can. Perhaps Mr Harris may be able to assist him. He does not expect to succeed in his first attempt, but the object is to secure the reversionary votes at the following election.

My best regards to all your family and love to the little Bride elect.

Believe me, my dear Mr Webber

Most Sincerely Yours,

F. Keating,

5th May

Editor's note...The writer of the above letter to Mr Webber (Senior) may be equated with the Mrs Keating referred to in the Journal entry for 8th September 1812. The letter probably dates from the period immediately before Waterloo and the 'success' was most likely Webber's posting to the RHA (D Troop). Sir Henry Phipps, Earl of Mulgrave, was the Master General of the Ordnance and responsible for postings. General Phipps was his brother.

It is probable that Mr Webber was living at this time at Lawhitton, which is near Stowford, where a Mr Harris of Hayne was the squire and thus may well have been in a position to influence the course of local democracy. The transmogrified and blooming boy was no doubt the Colonel's naval brother, George.

The spelling of 'Layndock' may provide an illustration of the pronunciation of those days. No light can be shed on other persons mentioned in the letter, so that the Uncle of Broad Street, old Ken, sweet Poll, Aunt Taylor and the little Bride elect may rest for the present incogniti.

II: A Memorial addressed to the Duke of Wellington

To: Field Marshall His Grace the Duke of Wellington, K.G., G.C.B., etc
The Memorial of Captain W. Webber of the Horse Artillery

Your memorialist earnestly entreats your Grace's favourable consideration of his peculiar case in the Battle of Waterloo added to his general services and trusts that it may please your Grace to recommend him for Brevet Rank [1] whenever an opportunity offers.

On the 18th June, 1815 your memorialist was 2nd Captain of Major Bean's Troop of Horse Artillery, and was wounded severely late in the action, a short time before his commanding officer was killed.

From this event, your memorialist became senior officer, though rendered incapable of acting in command, and as it devolved on a subaltern, no other claim of promotion for the service of that Troop which had been in five campaigns under your Grace's command, can be made. This your memorialist hopes will plead with your Grace for the favour now solicited and show that it cannot be deemed a precedent or a deviation from the principles of your Grace's recommendations.

From the preference your Grace was pleased to give to officers who had been a long time under your command, your memorialist has every reason to think he would have obtained the honor of your Grace's distinction had not his troop (from its just having arrived in England) been unattached to the orders of any general officer and thereby precluded from that support and recommendation other officers received and from which the services of the action might have been judged deserving and found, as your memorialist's claim was supposed

175

to be, to merit public notice.

Colonel Sir George Wood's list of recommendations was confined to officers actually commanding and the memorialist's name was therefore not included. In October, 1815, your memorialist had the honor of transmitting to your Grace a statement of his services together with the testimonies of Lieutenant-Generals Lord Hill and the Hon. Sir William Stewart. He has since received a letter from Lt-Colonel Sir Alexander Dickson of the Royal Artillery sanctioning your memorialist to request your Grace's reference to him 'as one who will testify most satisfactorily with regard to your memorialist's merit'. Your memorialist begs leave to add that he has been employed on service in the West Indies etc, etc.

III: Webber's Statement Of His Services [2]

My first Commission was dated 8th September 1803. I was soon after sent to the West Indies &, in the year following, from thence on an expedition to Surinam in South America, in the capture of which Colony I was actively employed the whole of the operations. I returned with the Army to the West Indies & remained there till an attack of yellow fever obliged me at the recommendation of a medical board to come to England.

I embarked at Barbados on board the *Duke of Cumberland* Packet & four days after was wrecked in a hurricane in St John's Bay, Antigua, by which misfortune I lost everything (with the exception of a few articles of trifling value) &, my ill health & debility having confined me to my bed till the ship was on the rocks & almost full of water, & being then exposed on the deck for many hours in the night in the rain & severity of the weather, & the sea making a complete breach over the vessel lying on her beam ends, I suffered very much, & my constitution received a shock from which it did not in the least recover till a long time after my arrival in England.

176

In 1806 I was appointed to the Horse Artillery and in 1808 served thro' the campaign in Spain under the late Sir John Moore. In April I was promoted to the rank of 2nd Captain & the next month joined the army in the Peninsula & served the four subsequent campaigns under the Duke of Wellington in Spain, the south of France & the Netherlands.

On the termination of the war in 1814 I went from Bordeaux to North America in command of a Brigade of Artillery with Major General Sir Manley Power's Division, & at the conclusion of the short campaign in Canada my health obliged me to come home.

In the June following I was appointed to the Horse Artillery & posted to the late Major Beane's Troop in time to accompany him to Flanders, & and joined the Army on the 17th June. The next day, in the battle of Waterloo, I was severely wounded & in consequence sent to Brussels & could not rejoin the Army till the beginning of August.

While under the Duke of Wellington I served three campaigns in Lord Hill's Corps & was in the battles of Vitoria, the Pyrenees, Orthez & Toulouse & in most of the actions & affairs in which that Corps, as the right wing of the Army was engaged.

When the Army was in position in the Pyrenees, four guns of Major Stewart Maxwell's Brigade of 9-Pdrs of which I was 2nd Captain, were placed in a redoubt on the summit of the Pass of Roncesvalles; a sudden & unexpected fall of snow in the night completely buried them before Lord Hill could be apprised of our situation. It was my turn of duty & orders were sent to the Field Officer commanding the post & to me to abandon the redoubt & the guns and to join the troops at Roncesvalles, which with the greatest difficulty we did.[3]

The next day Lord Hill requested me to make an attempt to return to the redoubt & to dismantle the guns & to render them of as little use to the enemy as possible. This I did, but having a hope that I might be able to recover them, I substituted wooden spikes for iron (with the same appearance) & buried the guns underground in such uncertain directions as not to be discovered except by the aid of some of my party, even when the return of warm weather might remove the snow.

I afterwards suggested to Lt-General the Hon Sir William Stewart (commanding the Division to which we were attached) a plan of sledges for recovering the guns & offered to use every effort to put it into effect if it met with his & Lord Hill's approbation; & I had every reason to expect success for the method tried, when a fortunate & only momentary change of weather enabled a working party of 500 men under a Field Officer to make a quick passage thro' the snow & to get the guns to Roncesvalles, 8 miles from the redoubt.

I do not presume to take any merit to myself for this act of mere duty, & should at the time, tho' going on favourably with the work, have been afraid it would not have been executed owing to the working party being so benumbed & dispirited by the intense cold, had not Lt-General Sir William Stewart made his way to us & with Major Maxwell & Lieut Calder (late of the Royal Sappers & Miners) succeeded in renewing the exertions of the men.

In stating thus minutely the circumstances of this service, by which Major Maxwell's Brigade of Artillery was again rendered complete - with the exception only of an ammunition wagon, limber, the round shot & some small stores at a most important period (the Army quitting their position & entering France) - my motive is to bring before the indulgent consideration of his Lordship, the Master General and the Hon'ble Board of Ordnance this additional trial of my constitution.

I went up to the redoubt, & was employed from morning till night, five days of the week [in which] the guns were abandoned, when it was deemed too severe a service for some of the party to go up twice, etc., etc.

Woolwich,
25th May, 1818

IV: The Medical Certificate

Brussels, November 6th, 1815
I certify that Captain W. Webber of the Royal Regiment of

Artillery has been attended by me here after the battle of Waterloo, where he received a violent contusion of his side by which blood in considerable quantities was caused to be vomited up and passed by stool for the period of a month after the injury, which was caused by his horse falling suddenly upon him, being knocked down when at full speed by a shell. The violence of the contusion, to judge from its effects, is likely to lay the foundation of future injury to his constitution.

James O. Bierne [?]
Assistant Surgeon Royal Artillery
(in charge of wounded officers)

V: A Second (undated) Memorial

Memorial of Captain William Webber of the Royal Horse Artillery
   His first Services were in the West Indies, in South America and in the campaign of 1808 under Sir John Moore in Spain. The last three campaigns in the Peninsula and the South of France he was 2nd Captain of a Brigade of Artillery attached to the 2nd Division of Infantry, in Lord Hill's Corps, and was in the battles of Vitoria, the Pyrenees and Toulouse, in the actions of St Palais and Sauveterre and in other affairs of less importance prior to these periods. From France he was sent to Canada in command of a Brigade of Artillery with Major General Sir Manley Power's Division, but the nature of the operations in that country disappointed the hopes with which he had flattered himself for the command, and ill health at last obliged him to return to England. He was soon after appointed to the Horse Artillery and joined the army in Flanders with Major Beane's Troop on the 17th June. In the battle of Waterloo he was severely wounded, etc.

VI: A Request To Sell Annuity

I obtained my commission in the Royal Artillery on the 8th September 1803 and three months after was sent to the West Indies. In 1804 I volunteered and was actually employed in the expedition to, and capture of Surinam in South America. I served the campaign of 1808 and 1809 in the Horse Artillery under the late Sir John Moore. I served the campaigns on 1812-13 and 14 under the Duke of Wellington and was in most of the actions in which the right wing of the army was engaged. In June 1814 I was sent in command of a Brigade of Artillery to North America and at the termination of hostilities there I returned home and was re-appointed to the Horse Artillery at the request of Lord Hill and the General of my Division, the Hon'ble Sir William Stewart. I went immediately after with the troop to Flanders and was in the battle of Waterloo. In January 1819 I was recommended by the Duke of Wellington for Brevet rank as 'A retrospect for services in the Field'.

In January 1837 I obtained the rank of Brevet Lt-Colonel and immediately afterwards, being then on unattached half-pay, made a general offer of my services and received an acknowledgement from Sir Fitzroy Somerset that my offer was recorded. In August 1826, as my health was then very much impaired, I availed myself of the privilege granted to a certain number of Artillery officers to retire on the unattached list. My wish now is to be allowed to sell my unattached annuity.

On the 28th of this month I shall be fifty nine years of age.

United Service Club,
Pall Mall,
May 22nd, 1846

ORGANIZATION OF THE 2ND DIVISION
1ST JANUARY 1812
GOC LT-GENERAL SIR ROWLAND HILL

1st Brigade (Maj-General K. A. Howard), 1/50th, 1/71st, 1/92nd
1 company 5/60th.
2nd Brigade (Colonel Byng), 1/3rd, 1/57th, 1st Provisional Battalion
(i.e. 2/31st and 2/66th combined), 1 company 5/60th.
3rd Brigade (Colonel Wilson), 1/28th, 2/34th, 1/39th, 1 company
5/60th.
General Ashworth's Portuguese Brigade.
In support: 2 brigades of Artillery (including Captain Maxwell's 9-Pdr
Brigade).
General Hamilton's Portuguese Division with a further 2 brigades of
Artillery. These, though not within the 2nd Division, formed part of
the detached force under the command of General Hill.

Subsequent changes in the organization:
1812
>   April 14, Tilson-Chowne appointed GOC 'under Hill'.
>   November 10, Cadogan replaced Howard in command of the 1st
>   Brigade, Howard being transferred to the 1st Division.

1813
>   General Sir William Stewart appointed GOC 'under Hill's
>   direction'.
>   Barnes replaced Cadogan in command of the 1st Brigade.
>   Wilson of the 3rd Brigade died in January and O'Callaghan of
>   the 39th assumed command until July, when General Pringle
>   was appointed.

These organizational details have, with permission, been taken from
Wellington's Army, 1809-1814 by Sir Charles Oman, recently
re-published by Greenhill Books.

NOTES

Preface

1. Became 8 Field Battery on 1 April 1947. Information about Webber's postings has been taken from the original monthly muster rolls and pay lists in the Public Record Office, London (War Office Series 10).

2. 7 Battalion RA had been formed with effect from 1 April 1801 from the disbanded Royal Irish Artillery and was still almost entirely Irish in composition.

3. The numbers in brackets after Royal Artillery officers are from Kane's list of officers. Webber's number was 1165.

4. Captain (Brevet Major) W. Wilson had been Commander Royal Artillery (CRA) on the expedition to Surinam, as Lt-Col Stehelin had been ordered to remain at Barbados.

5. Became 40 Training Battery RA in 1947 (A.C.I. 406).

6. RA Officers' Letter Book in the Public Records Office (WO55/1192 Ps 150/1.

7. Disbanded at Athlone on 28 February 1819 as Captain J. A. Clement's Coy, 7 Battalion RA.

8. Became 99 Light Anti-Aircraft Battery on 1 April 1948.

9. Is now V Battery RHA.

10. Is now C Battery RHA.

11. B Troop RHA was the only Artillery unit present at Sahagun.

12. A rank equivalent to that of the modern Captain and borne by the second in command of a company RA or a troop RHA.

13. This Company became 1 Company, 4 Battalion RA in January 1825 - 4 Bty, 7 Brigade RA in 1859 - 72 Company RGA in 1902 - 428 Bty RFA in 1918 - & 156 Bty RFA in 1919. In 1920 it was absorbed in 82 Bty RFA and so ceased to exist as a separate entity. Companies were not numbered within battalions until January 1825.

14. These muster rolls and pay lists are in the PRO, Series 10 No 912 (1812) & 976 (1813).

15. War Office 55/1223 Pages 301, 320 and 136.

16. A & D Troops were each armed with five 9-pdr guns and one 5.5-inch howitzer and were both allotted to the Reserve.

17. He was officially reported as 'Slightly wounded', but the medical certificate (see appendix) issued by the assistant surgeon in charge of wounded officers at Brussels suggests something more serious.

18. Webber remained as substantive 2nd Captain in the regiment and indeed was never made a Captain in the Royal Artillery.

19. Captain Alan Cavalié Mercer (1064) RHA succeeded Captain Beane in command of D Troop. Commissioned December 1799. Colonel Commandant, Woolwich, 1859. General 1865. Author of the celebrated *Journal of the Waterloo Campaign*.

20. F Troop RHA was redesignated E Troop in 1817 on the disbandment of D Troop. V Battery RHA was raised in 1900, and in 1901 was authorised to be considered as being D Troop reformed (AO 112/1901).

Part I

1. Previously Assistant Commissary who raised the Estremadura Legion in the Spanish Service. Became Lt-General in the Spanish army and was knighted.

2. Captain Stewart Maxwell RA (966) commanded the 9-Pdr Brigade manned by Captain Maxwell's Company 4 Bn RA. Promoted Major 4/6/1814. Order of the Bath. Died 1824/5 at Pau.

3. There is no Cathedral in Llerena. The church of Nuestra Sexone de Granada is probably meant.

4. Lt-Colonel William Henry Bunbury, 3rd Regiment, the Buffs. Author of Reminiscences.

5. The organization of the 2nd Division can be seen at the end of the notes.

6. An interesting comment. The general reaction of the Spaniards of the interior to the Constitution of 1812 was reputedly one of hostility.

7. General Ballesteros had been in command of the Army of Asturias when it was severely mauled by Ney and Kellermann in 1809. In 1812 he had engaged Soult energetically in the south, but was bitterly opposed to Wellington's appointment as Commander-in-Chief of the Allied forces, and disobeyed an order in October 1812 to march to Hill's assistance. After making a bid for supreme power on 23rd October, he was imprisoned in North Africa by the Cortes.

8. The Royals and the 3rd Dragoon Guards under Maj-General John Slade.

9. George Webber, Colonel Webber's younger brother, was an officer in the Navy.

10. This was in fact Victor's II Corps.

11. This account is confused. Medellin was in the French rear.

12. Colonel John Squires RE.

13. An Alcade or Alcaid is, according to Webster's dictionary of 1828, a governor, prefect, jailer or warden, and not to be confused with an Alcalde, who is a magistrate or judge. Webber has consistently used Alcade, and this spelling has been adhered to.

14. Captain (Brevet Colonel) Alexander Dickson RA (844). It was a source of irritation to Wellington that he was not authorised to promote officers of the Royal Artillery or Engineers, as their promotion was the concern of the Ordnance Board. He therefore had him appointed a Colonel in the Portuguese Army. He commanded the artillery at Vitoria. His detailed diaries have been published. He was promoted Lt-General in 1837 and was Director General Artillery, GCB, KCH. He died in 1840.

15. Captain G. Lifebure (867) of D Troop RHA, which became V Battery RHA in 1949. Became ill and died - October 1812.

16. Lt William Swabey (1327). Author of *Diary of Campaigns in the Peninsula for the years 1811-12-13*. Wounded in knee at Vitoria; repeated probing failed to extract the bullet. At battle of Toulouse. Retired 1825. Noted rider; 'Swabey's leap' remembered over brook near Salford, Bedfordshire. Well read, accomplished linguist, died 1872.

17. Maj-General Chowne had recently changed his name from Tilson. commanded the 2nd Division for a period in 1812.

18. Part of Captain Maxwell's Brigade of guns had taken part in the capture of the Almaraz forts on 19/5/1812.

19. 'B'... was in fact 2nd Lieutenant C. R. Baldock (1510). He remained on Maxwell's strength for the remainder of 1813 and retired on half pay on 8/11/1819. M... was of course Maxwell. Swabey's diary for 20 October 1812 mentions Lieut Baldock as follows: 'Being obliged to quarter myself with poor Baldock of Maxwell's Brigade, who has gone mad , I was allowed no rest all night, and nothing contented him but strutting about in my pelisse and overturning all the apples

etc that he met with in the streets'

20. The Sierra de Guadalupe is a good deal further south than this. Webber passed over it at Santa Cruz de la Sierra.

21. These remarks, while no doubt regretable, are not untypical of the attitude of soldiers campaigning in a foreign country, towards the manners and customs encountered there.

22. Lt G. B. Smyth (1299) A Troop RHA.

23. The present boundary line runs well to the west of Oropesa.

24. At present (1990) a motorway is being constructed across the site - many bones have been uncovered in the process.

25. This is the famous Alcazar de Toledo, which was besieged in the Spanish Civil War.

26. This is puzzling. Webber probably means the two Castiles (Old and New).

27. Several British writers state the opposite view - i.e. that the French made far more conquests than the British, notwithstanding the inferiority of their appearance, because the British were so arrogant and despised all they saw.

28. Captain Henry Goldfinch RE (1003), later Lt-General, KCB and Commandant RE.

29. This is the Casa de Labrador, a country retreat in the style of the Petit Trianon at Versailles.

30. Captain Hew Dalrymple Ross (890), commanding A Troop RHA - now A Bty (the Chestnut Troop) RHA. The Troop was attached to the Light Division. Ross was Adjutant-General at the time of the Indian Mutiny, and in 1867 was the first Gunner to become a Field-Marshal.

31. Lt G. J. Belson (1235) A Troop RHA.

32. 2nd Captain C. C. Dansey (1138), wounded 30/9/1812, and at Waterloo.

33. Lt Thomas Trotter (1183) of Captain Maxwell's Coy.

34. There were no 'other ranks' in the RE at this period. These were supplied by the Royal Military Artificers - which had become the Royal Sappers and Miners on 5/3/1813.

35. 2nd Captain Edward Whinyates (1002) D Troop RHA. Commanded the '2nd Rocket Troop' at Waterloo, where he was wounded. Colonel Commandant Woolwich 1855, General 1864, KCB, KH.

36.	Lt William Brereton (1258) D Troop RHA, later Lt-General Sir William Brereton.

37.	Assistant Surgeon James Ambrose (116), Ordnance Medical Department, attached D Troop RHA.

38.	i.e. by semaphore.

39.	Captain A. Tulloh RA (801), CB. He was currently Sir Rowland Hill's CRA. Made prisoner by the French in 1813 and escaped from Verdun.

40.	The Hon Edward Charles Cocks, sometimes styled Somers-Cocks, was one of Wellington's most skilled intelligence officers. He served in the 16th Light Dragoons (not the 15th as recorded here) and had joined the 79th Highlanders at the time of his death at Burgos on 8th October 1812. His correspondence has recently been published by Spellmount under the title *Intelligence Officer in the Peninsula.*

41.	Probably A Troop RHA.

42.	Major (Brevet Lt-Col) A. Duncan RA (740), killed at Seville 29/9/1812. Had been CRA at Cadiz.

43.	2nd Captain R. M. Cairns RA (1106) of Captain Dickson's Coy 10 Bn RA, disbanded 30/4/1817.

44.	2nd Captain W. Cator RA (1134) of Captain H. Owen's Coy 5 Bn RA, disbanded 30/1/1819.

45.	Ferdinand VII of Spain.

46.	Traditionally, the Saint's day or Santo was more important.

Part II

1.	Actually Colonel Skerret's Brigade - about 4,300 strong, which joined Hill's force from Cadiz.

2.	At the battles of Tamames and Ocaña in November 1809, the Spanish Army of La Mancha was destroyed as a fighting force, resulting some weeks later in the abdication of the Central Junta.

3.	In fact, Ballesteros was not there. See note 7 *Part I.*

4.	No record of this skirmish has been found elsewhere.

5.	i.e. the uprising of the Dos de Mayo in 1808.

6.	Whinyates was in temporary command of D Troop RHA (lately Lifebure's).

7.	Soult claimed 700 prisoners.

8.	These were the 47th and 95th Regiments.

9. Clerks of Stores Atkinson and Causton.
10. Possibly Lt-Colonel Raymond Pelly of 16th Light Dragoons.
11. Lt-Colonel W. Robe RA (654) was evacuated to England. Died of wounds at Waterloo.
12. At Arapiles, south of Salamanca.
13. 1st Bn Gordons.
14. 1st Bn Gloucesters.
15. Lt W. H. Bent RA (1449).
16. Captain (Brigade Major) R. Macdonald RA (858) commanding E Troop RHA.
17. General Sir Edward Paget.
18. Actually 10th Chasseurs à Cheval.
19. The guerrilla commander, Juan Palarsa, otherwise known as 'el Medico'.
20. Lt-Colonel George Julius Hartmann, King's German Legion Artillery.

Part III

1. Ensign W. Farquharson, 3rd Regiment, the Buffs.
2. High praise that is worth noting in view of the many complaints made elsewhere against the Spaniards.
3. Major George Gore, 9th Dragoons.
4. Lt-Colonel (Brevet Colonel) George Wilson, 39th Regiment (1st Bn Dorsets). Commanded 2nd Bde until his death in 1813.
5. Lt-Colonel Charles Stewart, 50th Regiment (1st Bn Queen's Own Royal West Kents).
6. Staff Surgeon Duncan Mackintosh.
7. This passage serves to amplify the description of the Cathedral surrounds in the Journal entry of 2nd December.
8. The allusion is not understood; the Spanish for fly is *mosca*.
9. Major J. H. Carncross RA (727), CRA to Hill.
10. On 14th May 1809 the bridge at Alcantara was defended by Colonel W. Mayne with 1st Bn the Loyal Lusitanian Legion, the Battery of the LLL, the Idanha-a-Nova Militia Regiment and 50 sabres of 11th Portuguese Cavalry Regiment against a large force under Marshal Victor.
11. Major Henry Sturgeon, Royal Staff Corps.
12. There is a detailed sketch of this bridge in the Wellington papers

at the University of Southampton.

13.   Lt Richard Litchfield RA (1453).

Part IV

1.   One division is a section of two guns.

2.   Lt George A. Moore RA (1410) embarked for the Peninsula in February 1813 in charge of drafts. He joined Captain T. Hutchesson's Coy 3 Bn RA.

3.   Lt Edward Jacob Bridges RA (1438), in Cairns' Brigade.

4.   Captain George Beane RHA (914), commanding D Troop RHA, formerly Lifebure's. Was Webber's commanding officer at Waterloo, where he was killed.

5.   Maxwell's Coy 4 Bn RA had been present at Albuera on 16/5/1811.

6.   General Francis Xavier de Castaños, 1756-1852. Had fought in Germany against Frederick the Great. Was present at the siege of Gibraltar, 1774-82. His Army of Andalucia forced Dupont's Corps to surrender at Baylen in 1808. In the winter of 1808-09 commanded the Army of the Centre, but was defeated by Lannes. Much respected by Wellington, with whom he collaborated closely at the siege of Badajoz and at Vitoria. Later appointed to Spanish Council of State.

7.   Captain (Brevet Lt-Colonel) John May RA (883) was Adjutant General in the Peninsula.

8.   Webber means the Council of Regency. The supreme Junta (properly the Supreme Central Junta of Government) was dissolved in 1810.

9.   Sir Thomas Graham became Lord Lynedoch but, contrary to this Journal entry, the 2nd Division was of course with that part of the army advancing on Salamanca (together with Alten's and Slade's cavalry, the Household Brigade, the Light Division, Campbell's Brigade of Portugese, the Spanish regiment of Julian Sanchez, and the Conde do Amarante's Portugese Division).

10.   Most British accounts speak quite highly of both the appearance and the performance of the Spanish troops employed in the campaign of 1813.

11.   The special significance of the term 'Brigade' as applied to the Artillery is explained in the preface.

12.   This place cannot be traced. Graham's forces crossed the Douro at

the ferries of São Jão de Pasqueira, Peso de Regua and Barca de Pocinho.

13. June 4th was the day celebrated in the Army as the King's birthday.

14. Pablo Morillo, commander of the 1st Division of the Fourth Army. In 1808 he was a sergeant.

15. Captain F. Glubb's Coy 5 Bn RA, manning an 18-pdr reserve brigade.

16. Refers to Gen Sir John Murray's abortive siege of Tarragona in early June 1813. Though vastly outnumbering the French he raised the siege when the fortress was on the point of surrendering and withdrew, leaving a Spanish force of 6,000 men to its fate to the North of Barcelona.

17. Lisbon was notorious for its filth.

18. Col O'Callaghan of 1/39th commanded the 3rd Bde from January to July 1813.

19. Gen Sir William Stewart, GOC 2nd Division 'under Hill's guidance' from 1813.

20. Captain (Brevet Major) R. W. Gardiner RHA (979), commanding E Troop RHA. Swabey's Diary reports that 'Gardiner's guns did great havoc and in Burgos were found sixty wounded with cannon shot and shrapnel shells, of which we made great use.'

21. Lt H. F. Cubitt RA (1310) joined Maxwell's Brigade on 1/4//1813 as replacement for Trotter.

22. Pancorvo was an imposing defensive position and had been an important base for the French in their struggle against the guerrillas.

23. It is believed, however, that the soldiers were deprived of their greatcoats as a consequence of having been issued with tents, and that subsequently they suffered considerably from this.

24. In 1813 the activities of the guerrillas paralysed much of Patriot Spain, and made it much harder to mobilise the Spaniards.

25. 'HQ Divisions and Hill's column moved, using all available secondary roads... by Villadiego and Montorio respectively, on the bridge of Puente Arenas. [They] had on 13, 14th and 15th very hard marches across upland roads where artillery had never been seen before'. Oman: *History of the Peninsular War*.

Appendix

1.   The award of a Brevet had generally been granted (upon recommendation) to 2nd Captains in the Artillery who had commanded
their units at Waterloo. General Sir William Stewart was not
perhaps the best advocate that could have been chosen; the Duke
once said of him 'He could never obey an order.' Sir Alexander
Dickson was a happier choice; see note 14, *Part I*.

2.   This is presumably a repetition of the 'Statement of his Services' that
he claimed he had sent to the Duke of Wellington in 1815 - see
preceding Memorial.

3.   The incident in the pass of Roncesvalles will have taken place during
the period end-October to first week in November 1813, when the
weather became so bad that it was physically impossible for Hill's
Division to move - they were up to their knees in snow. The weather
improved on 4th November.

Select Bibliography

Anderson, Joseph Jocelyn: *Recollections of a Peninsular Veteran*, London, 1913

Anglesey, George Charles Henry Victor Paget, Marquis of: *One-Leg; The Life and Letters of Henry William Paget, First Marquess of Anglesey, KG 1768–1854*, London, 1961

Bell, George: *Rough Notes by an Old Soldier, During Fifty Years Service, From Ensign G.B. to Major-General C. B . . .*, London, 1867. 2 vols

Blakeney, Robert: *A Boy in The Peninsular War, The Services, Adventures, and Experiences of Robert Blakeney, Subaltern in The 28th Regiment*. Edited by Julian Sturgis, London 1899; London, 1989

Brett-James, Antony: *Life in Wellington's Army*, London, 1972

Costello, Edward: *The Peninsular and Waterloo Campaigns*. Edited by Antony Brett-Janes, London, 1967

Dickson, Alexander: *The Dickson Manuscripts. Being Diaries, Letters, Maps, Account Books, With Various Other Papers. From 1809 to 1818.* Edited by Major John H. Leslie, Woolwich Royal Artillery Institution, 1908; Cambridge, 1987–91

D'Urban, Benjamin: *The Peninsular Journal of Major-General Benjamin D'Urban. . . 1808–1817.* Edited with an introduction by I. J. Rousseau, London and New York, 1930

Dyneley, Thomas: *Letters Written While on Active Service, 1806–15.* Woolwich, 1896; London, 1984

Fortescue, John W: *A History of The British Army*, London, 1910–30 19 volumes

Grattan, William: *Adventures of The Connaught Rangers, From 1808 to 1814*, London, 1847. 2 vols; London 1989.

Harris, *Recollections of Rifleman Harris*, London, 1829

Hughes, B. P.: *British Smooth-bore Artillery*, London, 1969

Kincaid, John: *Adventures in the Rifle Brigade, in The Peninsular, France and the Netherlands from 1809–1815*, London, 1847

Lachouque, Henry, Jean Tramie and J. C. Carmigniani: *Napoleon's War in Spain; The French Peninsular Campaign 1807–1814*, London, 1982

Myatt, Frederick: *Peninsular General: Sir Thomas Picton 1758–1815*, Newton Abbot, 1980

Napier, Sir William Francis Patrick: *History of the War in The Peninsula and in the South of France, From the Year 1807 to the Year 1814*, London, 1876. 6 vols

Oman, Charles William Chadwick: *A History of The Peninsular War*, Oxford, 1902–30. 7 vols

Rocca, Albert Jean Michel de: *In The Peninsula With a French Hussar*, London, 1990

Schaumann, August Ludolf Friedrich: *On the Road With Wellington; The Diary of a War Commissary in The Peninsular Campaign*. Edited and Translated by Anthony M. Ludovici, London, 1924

Swabey, William: *Diary of Campaigns in the Peninsula for the Years 1811–12–13: By an Officer of E Troop (Present Battery) Royal Horse Artillery*. Edited by Col. A. W. Linyets RHA, Woolwich, 1895; London, 1984

Ward, Stephen George Peregrine: *Wellington's Headquarters: A Study of the Administrative Problems in The Peninsula, 1809–1814*, London, 1957

Weller, Jac: *Wellington in the Peninsula, 1808–14*, London, 1962

Wellington, Arthur Wellesley, 1st duke of: *The Dispatches of Field Marshal the Duke of Wellington During His Various Campaigns in India, Denmark, Portugal, Spain, the Low Countries, and France from 1799 to 1818*. Compiled from the official documents, by Lieut. Col. Gurwood, London, 1837–39. 13 vols

Wellington, Arthur Wellesley, 1st duke of: *General Orders*, London, 1811–14. 5 vols

Index

Abrantes, hosp, 100; depôt, 137, 141
Alcantara, description of, 136
Alten, Gen Victor, 132, 139
Amarante, Conde do, 144, 149, 151
Ambrose, Asst Surgeon 29, 87 & n.
Aranjuez, 77, 83–7; evacuated, 98
Arapiles, battle site, 109, 111
Aravaca, position on heights, 101–2
Army Organization, 35, 36
Armies/Army Corps: Allied, 35, 93, 151,
    157; Hill's, 43, 139, 150, 162, 165,
    177; French, 41, 93, 158; Spanish,
    151–3, 151–5
Artificers' Corps, 84
Artillery: Ammunition, 38, 91, 102,
    109, 115; Drivers, 36, 69, 88, 100,
    129, 131; Equipment, 36–7, 47, 68,
    118, 123, 130; Organization, 36,
    37
  Royal (Foot) Artillery: Companies, 31–3,
    35, 104, 117, 142, 153–4, 157, 158,
    186 n43 & n44, 188 n2; Capt
    Maxwell's Bde, W. joins, 35; Zafra,
    43; Trujillo, 56; Almaraz, 62;
    Talavera, 70; Toledo, 73; Aranjuez,
    77; Aravaca, 103; Alba de Tormes,
    108; Arapiles, 112; winter quarters,
    123; W. commanding, 128; Hill
    inspects, 144; Alba de Tormes, 148;
    outside Burgos, 162; Puente Arenas,
    170; Vitoria, Roncesvalles, invasion of
    France, 177; Canada, 39, 177;
    subsequent history, 182 n13
  Royal Horse Artillery: 33–6; Troops, A,
    89 & 186 n41, 182 n16; B, 33; C,
    33–4; D, 33, 174, (Lifebure's), 60–1,
    95, 100, (Whinyates'), 103 & n, 112,
    116, 124, 137, (Beane's), 142, 149,
    175, 177, 179, 182 n16, 183 n20; E,
    183 n20; F, 40, 183 n20; Gardiner's
    163; Rocket Troop, 185 n35. Also,

65–6, 68, 77, 79, 89, 95, 108,
    112–13, 123, 158, 163–4, 177
  French, 103, 111, 116, 163; German,
    120; Portuguese, 55, 61–2, 64,
    65–6, 87, Col Tulloh's 88; 99, 109,
    127, 128
  Officers: Baldock, Lt C. R., 65, 100,
    124; Beane, Capt George, 28, 40,
    142, 149, 175; Belson, Lt G., 80;
    Bent, Lt W., 116; Bridges, Lt E, 142;
    Cairns, Capt R., 89, 142, 152–4;
    Carncross, Maj J., 135; Cator, Capt
    W., 89, 117; Cubitt, Lt H., 164;
    Dansey, Capt C., 83; Dickson, Gen
    Sir A., 57, 173, 176; Duncan, Col
    A., 89; Evelegh, Capt, 34; Fraser,
    Capt H., 33; Frith, Lt, 53; Gardiner,
    Maj R., 163; Glubb, Capt F., 182
    n15; Gold, Capt C., 33; Hawker,
    Capt J., 35; Hutchesson, Capt T.,
    188; Jenkinson, Lt. G., 143; Laws,
    Col M., 24, 31; Lifebure (Lefebure),
    Capt G., 60–1, 95, 100; Litchfield,
    Lt R., 137, 141; Macdonald, Maj,
    116; Martin, Capt W., 35; Maxwell,
    Capt S., see 'M'; Mercer, Capt C., 28,
    183; Moore, Lt G., 142; Owens, Capt
    H., 186; Robe, Col W., 106; Ross,
    Maj Hew (later Fd Marshal), 80;
    Sheldrake, Capt J., 31; Smyth, Lt G.,
    68, 79, 80, 82, 87, 88, 142–3;
    Stehelin, Col E., 31; Swabey, Lt W.,
    60; Timbers, Brig K., 25; Trotter, Lt
    T., 83, 110, 128, 131; Tulloh, Col
    A., 88, 127-8, 153; Webber, Capt
    W., see 'W'; Webber-Smith, Capt J.,
    40; Whinyates, Capt (later Gen) E.,
    28, 87, 89, 103, 112, 116, 124, 137;
    Wilson, Capt W., 32, 182
Arundell family, 23, 26
Ashworth, Col C., 110–11, 162, 181

193